Made it
THROUGH
the
STORM

Made it
THROUGH
the
STORM

SAMANTHA WILLIAMS

XULON PRESS

Xulon Press
2301 Lucien Way #415
Maitland, FL 32751
407.339.4217
www.xulonpress.com

Paperback ISBN-13: 978-1-6312-9633-8

Ebook ISBN-13: 978-1-6312-9634-5

God has a plan.
"Be still and know that I am God".
(Psalm 46:10)

Disclaimer

THE NAMES IN this book have been changed to protect the anonymity of any and all persons involved aside from myself and Alisha "Lish" Curry.

Acknowledgments To:

Lindsey Robison, who helped me realize that I had a story to tell... Because of you, I've found the courage to share my truth.

My best friend, Alisha Curry. I want to thank you for pushing me, motivating me, supporting me, and encouraging me to continue writing. Thank you for being my friend and my sister. I'm so proud of all that you've accomplished!

Thibaut, thank you for loving me unconditionally. When I first shared my story with you, you didn't take pity on me, nor did you judge me; Instead you respected me even more. You kissed my scars and helped me heal. You saw the real me and encouraged me to continue to live, to write, and to share my story with the world. I love you more than you could ever know, and I am beyond thankful to have you in my life. I thank God for you every day.

Danaé Reid. You have helped me turn my testimony into a story and have been so patient and understanding throughout this entire process. I know it wasn't easy. I thank you for editing my story and dedicating your time to helping me share my journey.

To my cousin Ryan Riley thank you for drawing the cover to my book, I gave you an idea that I had, and you brought my vision to life.

GUIDE ME IN your truth and teach me, for you are God my Savior and my hope is in you all day long. (Psalms 25:5)

Table of Contents

Introduction

My name is Samantha Williams, and this is my testimony. People often believe that they know my story, but they only know about a fraction of what I've endured. I hope that you're able to use these anecdotes as a means of inspiration. Allow my words to guide you, to help you, and to encourage you. If I can make it through the storm, so can you.

God led me to write this book. I feel compelled to remit my testimony so that I might help others overcome their individual trials and tribulations… This book is for those who've been depressed, betrayed, sexually assaulted, physically harmed, and mentally abused. I know that God's grace is the reason that I made it through, and I know that his unchanging hand will help you do the same.

I was raped at the age of 16. The experience was traumatic and ultimately scarred me to the point that I no longer believed that the word "no" had any power. As a result of my brokenness, I became promiscuous and would frequently allow myself and others to disrespect my body and my mind. Everything I subconsciously knew I should say "no" to, I did not.

The physical and mental abuse I endured during that period of time filled me with hatred, sadness, and anger. For a while, I'd thought that I deserved all of the obscenities that were casted my way, but that notion eventually vacated my psyche when I realized that I was worth much more than anyone was giving me credit for.

I came to realize that I was actually fighting my trauma instead of working to heal. After a while, I could no longer stand for it. I was broken then, and to an extent, I still am. However, God's love has allowed me to find the beauty in my pain.

One night when I was at my lowest, I cried and pleaded with God that he would forgive me for my sins and my ignorance. I needed him to free me from the Hell I was living in. I begged him to heal my soul and my body, and my life has been much better since then.

Before I could learn to love myself again, I felt that I needed to forgive my abuser for all that he'd done. In that, I knew that I was also making the decision to give all of my hurt over to God. I allowed him to fight the battle for me and he allowed me to come out of it triumphant.

My decision to rededicate my life back to Christ was the best and easiest choice I've ever made. I was ready to change. And even though no one knew what I was going through, God did, and because of that, he redirected my course indefinitely...

Know that I am no angel... I was not happy with myself for quite some time; But God. He has pulled me through many storms and has allowed me to see the other side. I didn't see it then, but I now understand that God has always been by my side, emitting light in an otherwise dark space.

Since putting Jesus first, my life has been filled with blessings, joy, new beginnings and personal growth. Allow my life to be a reminder to walk by faith, and not by sight. Be still and trust him... Welcome to what my life looked like before the storm.

WHEN I LOST hope, God gave me faith. The Lord is my Shepherd. I have all that I need. (Psalm 23:1) (NIV)

Letter To Myself

To the girl I used to know, I know you thought you were alone on this journey, but now you see that you never were. There are so many girls just like you in this world. I'm excited for us to walk down this path together and reflect on everything that we've been through and learned along the way. You have been given the gift of a big heart, which can sometimes be your downfall, but I want you to always recognize it as an asset. Take heed, but never allow this world to turn you cold.

I pray that you never forget to look in the mirror to fix your crown. Remember that you are beautiful, and that self-validation is more than enough. As a child of the King, never forget that your light shines so bright and that you are never to dim it.

Your attempt to grow will intimidate some people, but never allow that to deter you. Falling into this trap will only result in the blocking of your own blessings. Respect your body and your mind enough to make the right decisions for you. God's love and acceptance is all the external approval you need. Continue to want more. Take every failure as a lesson.

I am proud to be the beautiful God-Fearing Woman that I've become. Continue to pray and be obedient. Appreciate where you've come from because it has made you the woman that you are today. Your struggles have made you strong and fearless. Everything you've made it through has taught you that no matter what happens, you will come out stronger on the other side.

SUBMIT TO GOD resist the devil. And he will flee (James 4:7)

CHAPTER 1

Where the Skeletons Hung

WHEN YOU FOLLOW the desires of your sinful nature the results are very clear: sexual immorality, impurity, lustful pleasures, idolatry sorcery, hostility, quarreling, jealousy, outbursts of anger, selfish ambition, dissension, division, envy, drunkenness, wild parties, and other sins like these. Let me tell you again, as I have before, that anyone living that sort of life will not inherit the -kingdom of God.
-Galatians 5:19-21 NLT

I am an ordinary girl from West Oak Lane, Philadelphia. For a while, life had been very kind to me, but it seemed that everything changed around the time I transferred to Martin Luther King High School.

My downward spiral all began with my childhood best friend, Jasmine. Her and I did nearly everything together, but our relationship suddenly changed once I transferred schools. While outwardly, she seemed to be happy for this new step that I was taking, I began to suspect that she was secretly jealous of me.

To give some context, I was labeled a "hoe" even prior to losing my virginity. Initially I wasn't bothered by this because I knew it wasn't true, however, I wasn't sure why or how people got that idea. Eventually, it was brought to my attention that Jasmine was the one who spread the rumors, but because she was my best friend, I initially didn't believe that she was the one speaking ill of me… I later found out that it was in fact true.

The truth is, I knew my friend was leaning towards the side of promiscuity, and I'd always heard the saying "you are the company you keep because they are a reflection of you", but I never thought too much of it because I loved her. I didn't care what she did because I thought it had no effect on my life, but I was wrong.

I started dating a new guy, whose name I will redact as to protect his anonymity, but we used to talk fairly often, and I really thought he liked me. Yet, after he got what he wanted from me, I realized that he'd only been giving me attention because of the rumors he'd heard, and because I was so close with Jasmine, who was considered a "hoe" herself.

Two days later, I saw that guy and a new girl holding hands. That girl was his girlfriend and had been the entire time. To make matters worse, people were beginning to find out that we'd had sex. I was left in a state of hopelessness and disappointment because I believed that I should have known better, but I also knew that I couldn't change what'd happened.

Understandably, I distanced myself from my then best friend, and kept to myself and my other small circle of friends, but this upset her. As a means to hurt me, she started spreading more vicious rumors about me... Rumors that landed me in more trouble than I could've imagined.

Once the smoke cleared from that incident, I started seeing another man named Troy. Troy and I had always been friends, but we eventually took our relationship a step further. I can recall one day that we were hanging out in the park, just talking, and he reassured me that he didn't believe any of the rumors that he'd heard about me. I was so happy to hear that someone believed in me that I wanted to cry tears of joy... My feelings for Troy deepened, but I quickly learned that adding benefits to an already established friendship can be dangerous, and in my case, it complicated things beyond repair. I wanted a relationship with him, but he wasn't interested. Ultimately, I came to the conclusion that he was using me, even though I knew that he would never admit to it.

The discovery of Troy's true intent hurt my feelings because he'd always been there for me. Someone close to both of us shed light on who Troy really was and that he'd had a girlfriend the whole time. When I confronted him, he reassured me that they were broken up, but I later found that, that was a lie. I respected him for his honesty, but I had to end it there because once again, I found myself catching feelings for someone who was only in it for the sex. I eventually realized that he was never really my friend and ended it, but I couldn't put all the blame on him for his actions; I had the Jezebel spirit embedded in me, and I wasn't even aware.

A few weeks had gone by at this point... I was late for school and due to my tardiness, I had to go to what was called the late room. One of my fellow classmates shouted, "why don't nobody like you?!" at me, and all I could do was sit there. I blocked out the comment because after all I'd been through, I no longer cared about what people thought of me. I took in all of the rumors and I allowed them to turn me into a careless person. Initially, I thought that a nonchalant attitude would fix all my problems, but in reality, I was broken and lost. I hated myself and that hatred turned me into something I wasn't, but to the world, this was the new me.

Some time had passed before I started hanging out with Jasmine again. And with that, I started smoking, lying to my mom about where I was, saying that I was staying at Jasmine's when I was really spending the night with a boy named Sean.

Sean and 'I relationship was never serious, but I was consciously engaging in a meaningless, sexual relationship with him. I didn't realize that I'd been signing a "soul tie contract" at the time, but I was. I was naïve and believed all the lies that men had told me; Not realizing that this was a means to mask how hurt I really was. I took to opening my legs for the men because I craved the attention and love that I felt was lacking.

3

Lesson

That situation with Troy, no matter how painful it might've been, showed me for the first time that I should never settle for less, and that being someone's "friend with benefits", can only lead to pain. However, this wouldn't be the last time that I learned this.

BUT COWARDS, UNBELIEVERS, the corrupt, the murderers, the immoral, those who practice witchcraft, idol worshipers, and all liars-there fate is in the fiery lake of burning sulfur. This is the second death.
-Revelation 21:8 NLV

CHAPTER 2

Family "Love"

BUT THOSE WHO won't care for their relatives, especially those in their own household, have denied the true faith. Such people are worse than unbelievers. –1 Timothy 5:8 NLT

When I was in the 10th grade, my mother and I had gotten evicted, and we'd only found out because one day after school, I noticed that my key wouldn't work. In a panic, I called my mom, and informed her of my dilemma and she advised me to go to my brother Terrell's house. That's where we'd found out. I wasn't interested in staying with them, but I knew we had no other option. I was heartbroken and once again, left lost and hopeless.

Moving in with my brother and his family added extra stressors to my life and made everything much worse... It's important to note that my brother and I have had our fair share of ups and downs and I certainly wouldn't say that we were close. He has always viewed me as his little sister and would try to control my life because of it.

Ironically, the house that we were staying in once belonged to my parents, but my mother allowed Terrell and Shana to have the house years prior to this incident for multiple reasons.

Upon moving back into our old home, I had hoped to reclaim my old room, but my brother and Shana wanted their son Tyron to have it, even though he never slept in that room to begin with. They'd given my mother and I a small room to share instead. I didn't understand why he was doing this to me. To us. But we had no other choice.

Because the room was so small, I figured that it wouldn't be an issue if I'd left my clothes in Tyron's closet, but Terrell did not like that. In retaliation, he took my clothes out of the closet and put them in the trash bags and boxes... At the moment, all I could say was okay, but on the inside, I was fuming. I thought to myself, "I can't wait until the day that my mom says that we no longer have to live with them", and I meant it.

Within the first two weeks we stayed with them, Shana and I bumped heads fairly often. We would constantly bicker about the most trivial things, but even still, I genuinely thought she was cool. She was like family. However, after the constant bickering and the incessant discomfort, I could no longer stand being in that house. As a result, I began bouncing from house to house, including Jasmine's, Sean's, and eventually Troy's.

As previously noted, mine and Troy's relationship had soured, but I still looked at him as my "go-to" person. At this point, he was no longer with his girlfriend, and we once again crossed the boundaries of friendship. I somehow convinced myself that this time was different even though I knew deep down that it wasn't.

One night, during our stay, I got into an intense argument with my brother, and I called Troy crying. If I wasn't arguing with Shana, I was arguing with Terrell. Whenever I'd call Troy for comfort, he'd say, "Sam stop crying and getting so worked up. I'm always here for you. Shana is probably just jealous of you... You're stronger than this. And don't let your brother get to you", but the reminder never stopped feeling good. Once again, he felt like the only person who really understood me. I appreciated his support immensely and began to fall for him again. This time though, I knew that this relationship was going to be strictly physical.

Back at home, my personal life was rapidly getting worse. The environment was volatile, and I began to see another side of my brother that I didn't like. Him and Shanda weren't thoughtful and would place excess blame, judgement, and housework on me. I couldn't deal with our living arrangement anymore... This was no longer a place I could recognize as my home.

During the time we were staying with Terrell and his family, my mother had fallen ill which resulted in a multi-day stint in the hospital, and being that I still lived at home, I had no choice but to be under the watchful eyes of Terrell and Shana. Day after day, they became more controlling.

Tired and frustrated, I decided to go down the street to hang out with Jasmine for a couple of hours, but as I was gearing up to leave, Shana called out to me, "where are you going?" I wasn't sure why, but when I told her, she demanded that I be home no later than 8 pm. I hadn't even had a curfew...

Terrell chimed in behind her, "You heard what Shana said. If you are not back by 8 pm, you won't be coming into this house. We will lock you out.".

I tried to brush it off while I walked to Jasmine's house, but I couldn't. I felt like an enemy in my own "home". My brother's actions/inactions took a toll on me, and the fact that he allowed Shana to blatantly disrespect my mother and I despite all that we'd done to help them in the past was baffling and quite deplorable. In this, I learned that people will not always reciprocate the kindness that you show them.

In an effort to "keep the peace", I decided to stay in the house and chill one day so that there'd be no reason for them to bark at me, except for when I got up to run to the corner store. As always, Shana was breathing down my back, asking me where I was going, but this time I didn't respond... When I got back home from the store, the door was locked. I banged, no one answered. I peeked through the window and saw Shana sitting on the couch watching tv, but she wouldn't open the door for me. Finally, my mom opened the door and asked why I was banging on the door the way I was, to which I responded "Shana locked me out! She knew I was knocking on the door and she just sat there like she didn't hear me."

I walked in the house, looked at Shana, and something in me snapped.

"Really Shana you're going to lock me out! How petty can you be?"

"Yea I locked you out! I spoke to you and you didn't speak back."

My brother heard the ruckus and came to Shanda's rescue as he always did. His solution to solving the problem was pushing me up the steps.

"Ignore her Shana, she isn't nobody."

At this point, my mom also got involved and yelled at him to stop pushing me and not to put his hands on me… I thought the worst of it was over, but again, I'd been proven wrong. The day after the altercation, I came home from work and Terrell and Shana were sitting on the couch. Mocking me, Shana spoke as I walked up the steps. I didn't say anything because I knew her intent.

"Stop speaking to her! Stop trying to kiss her butt, she isn't nobody for you to be kissing her butt that is why she's going to die alone.", my brother yelled.

I was taken back by this. No one had ever said anything like that to me before, and I was hurt to my core by his words.

That night, I laid in bed alone, and cried myself to sleep, paralyzed by the thought that I would die alone and that no one would care. I couldn't believe my own flesh and blood could say such a thing to me. He couldn't love me… right? He certainly didn't like me.

About a month later, things at home had gotten worse. The house was already crowded as is but got even worse after Shana allowed her friend Jessica to move in as well.

Rebellious and a little bit spiteful, I decided to leave school early one day with a guy that I was talking to, just to hang out. We went back to my house, a few moments later, Jessica had walked in, looked at me and then left to make a phone call. Next thing I knew, my phone was ringing. It was my mom, calling me from work, asking me whether or not I'd had a boy over which I responded "yes", because there was no reason to lie since she'd known he was there.

My mother was pissed off by Shana's accusations. According to her and Jessica, she caught me having sex on the steps in the house. This of course wasn't true.

She'd recounted her conversation with Shana with me, "You're disrespectful... That's not even your house, that is still my house. I was nice to let you and Terrell stay there! You don't have a pot to piss in or a window to throw it at. You called me to get smart... remember who you are talking to! Why would Samantha be having sex on the steps when anybody could walk in the house at any moment? That doesn't make any sense! Did you see it with your own eyes? No! You are taking the word of your friend. She's lying because she knows that you don't like Samantha.... I don't trust her, nor do I trust you... but you don't have to worry about Samantha".

When my mom came home, she told me to pack my stuff because my dad would be around to pick me up. She didn't want me to stay there any longer because it was clear that I wasn't wanted there... I had no choice but to stay with my father.

THOSE WHO BRING trouble on their families inherit the wind. The fool will be a servant to the wise -Proverbs 11:29 NLT

CHAPTER 3

New Beginnings

THROW OFF YOUR old sinful nature and your former way of life, which is corrupted by lust and deception. Instead let the spirit renew your thoughts and attitudes. Put on your new nature, created to be like God truly righteous and holy. -Ephesians 4:22-24 NLT

About a month after I moved in with my father, my mother decided that she could no longer withstand living with my bother either... My parents had been separated for a while at the time, but once she moved in with us, her and my dad decided to get back together and buy a new house.

Living with my brother allowed me to build a closer relationship with my sister. I began to confide in her, and she did the same with me. One day while we were talking, I showed my sister a journal entry I'd written about myself. The entry talked about how I'd turned into someone that I wasn't as a result of the rumors, how one of the men I was talking to had given me Chlamydia, and how I blamed myself for everything I'd endured.

My sister sat me down, told me to wipe my eyes and assured me that I didn't need to cry.

"Don't let the rumors give the verdict of who you are as a person. You made some mistakes, yes, but are you going to let it define you as a person or are you going to brush it off? It's not the end of the world, and you will get through this, just be more careful".

After our conversation, I sat back and thought to myself, and I realized that she was right… I can't care about what people think of me and I can't let my mistakes define me or else I would remain stagnant. I needed to face all of my problems head on instead of running from them and allowing their thoughts to turn me into the very thing that they said I was. I needed change.

The month before summer break, I was walking to class, I'd ran into Winter, an old friend from the drill team that I hadn't seen in a while because of our conflicting schedules.

"What are you doing here?", I asked, excited to see her.

"This is my class, what are you doing here?"

"This is my class too! How is it that this is both our class and we never see each other?"

We talked for a while and I learned that she'd been suspended; That paired with the fact that I'd been skipping that class was the explanation behind why we hadn't crossed paths… It felt good to talk to her. She was refreshing and acted as a nice distraction from all of the other nonsense that was going on in my personal world.

We began to hang out every day, but a part of me was curious as to why she was interested in hanging out with me due to the perfuse rumors. I asked her why she didn't mind, and she told me that she didn't care because she was her own person and that she didn't think ill of me. She reminded me that regardless of whether you are good or bad, people are going to talk about you.

Hanging out with her was always great because she was goofy and always made me laugh.

The school year was coming to a close and I couldn't wait to spend the summer with my new friend. Because she'd had to go to summer school that year, our plans were always a bit delayed, but once she got out, she came right to my house and we had a blast. She would always make us Chicken Flavor Ramen Noodles with shrimp in it because it was her specialty, but it was so good! That summer seemed like it was going to be great, and I finally felt like I was gaining some control over my life.

CHAPTER 4

August 2005

BUT HE REFUSED to listen to her, and since he was stronger than she, he raped her. -2 Samuel 13:14 NIV

The summer of 2005 turned out to be the worst summer of my life. In the beginning, Winter and I would go to parties and really made an effort to make it the best summer yet and it was for a while, but that all changed on Tuesday August 16, 2005.

My cousin, Ari had came over to see me because she needed to get out of the house and wanted to have some fun. I'd had nothing planned that day, except that I'd told a girlfriend of mine that I would walk her to the bus stop later that day so she could see her boyfriend.

Ari came with me, and as promised and waited with my friend so that she didn't have to stand alone. Afterwards, Ari and I were walking back to my house when we saw a man driving by. He yelled out the window, "I know y'all feet hurt", and we started laughing, but kept walking and talking.

He finally passed us but quickly made a U-turn and pulled over beside us so that he could introduce himself to us

"Do y'all want a ride"?

"What's your name?", I asked.

"Dollar".

We got in his car and he drove us to the block I lived on and randomly asked if we wanted to go swimming. I didn't want to go because I didn't want to get my hair wet, but Ari didn't want to go in the house. I knew I couldn't leave her alone, so I decided that we could go with him and his two friends to the impromptu pool party.

He drove up to Sharpnack St and we ran into Jahlil, who was one of our mutual friends. Dollar and Jahlil began talking, but when he saw me, he started laughing and I joined in. The laughter eventually ended, and I told him I'd call him later that night.

Once the conversation was through, Dollar drove us to a nearby apartment that he knew had a pool. He claimed to live there, but something just didn't feel right and I was officially ready to go home…

When your gut is telling you, something is wrong, always go with your gut feeling because it is always right.

Dollar parked the car and told everyone to get out except for me. I asked him why he'd told everyone else to get out, and he said it was because he wanted to talk to me alone.

Ari walked over to me and asked me what was wrong, to which I responded that something felt off to me and I wanted to leave. I tried to be a team player since I knew she was having a good time, but she understood how I'd felt and obliged.

Finally.

We were gearing up to leave, but Dollar asked that I ride to the store with him, and then promised that he would take me home afterwards. I asked Ari to come with us, but he told her no.

Naively, I got in the car and we drove off, but I noticed that he'd already passed by two corner stores.

"What store are you going to?" I asked, confused and concerned.

"That is not the store I want to go to. The one I like is down the street… Can you sit back and ride? What's the harm in me wanting to get to know you? I asked you to ride with me so I could talk to you.", he replied.

He started asking me personal question like, "how did I know Jahlil" and "did I have sex with him". Before I could even answer any of his questions, he pulled up onto a random street, parked the car, and looked at me…

"I want to have sex".

"No!" I said,

"Why?"

I couldn't believe that he had the audacity to question my choice. He was so mad at my decision that he forced me to get out of his car.

"I don't know where I'm at, can I at least use your phone?"

I tried calling Ari at first, but I didn't know her number by heart. I then tried calling my house, thinking that my mom or dad would answer the call, but the call wouldn't go through… That's when I noticed that his phone was off. He knew and didn't say anything.

"Either you let me hit or get out", he said.

I got out of the car and slammed the door and he quickly drove off, but then backed the car up and said, "get in I was only playing with you. I'm going to take you back to your cousin and then take y'all home."

Again, I didn't listen to my intuition.

I got back in the car, but I got in the back seat instead of the front. Hoping that he'd really take me home this time, and the only thing he said was, "I want to have sex". I tried to open the car door, but he locked it before I could open it. He grabbed me and jumped in the back seat. I tried to fight him off so I could get out, but he was much stronger than me. I screamed, I cried, I begged him please, "please don't do this"! I cried, I yelled "NO!" … He punched me in the stomach, pushed me down against the seat, pulled my pants off, and told me to "shut the hell up or he would kill me".

"Stop crying, you know you want it."

He punched me again as I tried to push him off me.

"Stop fighting it!", he demanded.

He was holding my arms above my head and forced himself inside of me. I could feel my stomach turning into knots. I felt disgusted.

17

I couldn't stop crying. I couldn't believe this was happening to me. My worst fear was happening and there was nothing I could do about it. I closed my eyes and kept telling myself "This is just a dream. This is just a dream", but every time I opened my eyes, there he was. On top of me.

"Stop crying. You know you like it. You know you wanted it".

All I could do in that moment was pray for it to be over and pray that he wouldn't kill me.

"Turn around" he yelled. I wouldn't. I couldn't. My body was frozen. When he finally finished, he gave me my pants and he apologized. I got up, wiped my eyes, put my pants on, and got out of the car. I didn't know where I was, but at that moment, I didn't even care. I had to get away from him, so I started walking.

"Get back in the car" he said as he grabbed my wrist.

"Don't touch me... you raped me!" I screamed.

"I'm sorry, I didn't mean to. Please don't tell anybody. I will pay you if you don't tell anyone. How much do you want?"

That moment kept playing in my head like a broken record. I couldn't speak. I couldn't move. I couldn't believe it. I blamed myself. I'd done so much work to fix myself and here I was, broken again.

We returned to the apartment shortly after even though it had felt like a million years. I'd put my sunglasses on so that I could hide my tears... I didn't want Ari to see my face.

When we pulled up, the first thing Ari said was, "that was a long ride to the store". Dollar laughed and replied, "we weren't gone that long". I sat there in silence.

Ari could tell that something was wrong and kept asking, but I ignored her. I knew that if I talked, I would cry.

"What's wrong?" she asked incessantly.

"She's fine. Why do you keep asking her what's wrong?", Dollar said.

He tried to grab my hand, but I moved it away quicker than he could blink.

"I'm not talking to you I'm talking to my cousin and I know something is wrong with her!" Ari said.

After some back and forth, Dollar finally dropped us off. I scurried out of the car so fast and started power walking home even though I really wanted to run.

I suddenly felt Ari's firm grasp on my arm.

"Don't touch me!" I exclaimed as I continued to walk down the street.

"Sam. Samantha, talk to me. What's wrong"

"Nothing".

"It is Samantha. You're too quiet and acting different...What happened?" I just kept walking. I was trying to hurry up and get home.

During my trek home, Jahlil spotted me, but noticed something was wrong when I walked by without acknowledging him.

He grabbed me, held me against the car and took off my sunglasses.

"What's wrong? Why are you crying? What happened?"

"He raped me".

Ari ran over to me and entrapped me in her arms. "Why didn't you tell me? Why didn't you say anything in the car", she asked?

Jahlil reacted to my admission by punching the car and then he made phone calls.

"Sam get up, come on you gotta get up."

He walked me home and stood outside while I walked in the house.

I went in my room and laid down pulled my pillow closer to me, and Ari came in right behind me.

"Sam you need to tell your parents. You can't keep this from them".

Suddenly she disappeared.

I overheard her talking to my mother in the other room.

"Cousin Jackie, Sam wants you. She wants to talk to you"

My mom came into my room and asked me what was wrong.

19

I'd felt a foreign pain as my mom walked in my room. How was I supposed to look her in the eyes and tell her what happened to me… that I was raped? How?

I was sitting on the bed when my mom bent down to look me in the face. Ashamed and scared, I hid my face with my pillow.

"Why are you crying? What is wrong? You can tell me"

I looked her in the eyes and screamed, "I was raped!"

I could feel her heart drop and could see the pain welling up in her eyes. She began to cry and started yelling for my father. "Bobby. Call the cops!"

She looked at me and said, "don't take nothing off" … At this point, my father was crying too.

The police officers came over and asked me a slew of questions and took my report. That night we revisited the scene of the crime and I was taken to the hospital as well.

I immediately blamed myself. I kept thinking "I said NO, but he still did it". My no meant nothing to him. "How could I let this happen? I should have known not to get in the car with him especially when something was telling me not to". My loved ones kept trying to reassure me that it wasn't my fault, but I didn't believe them. It was my fault. I felt dirty, ashamed, and scared.

For weeks, I couldn't go outside unless I was with my parents. If I did decide I felt comfortable to go outside by myself, it was only to the front steps. I wouldn't leave from my front door. Even though the police caught him, I just couldn't bring myself to leave. However, that all changed one day when Winter came by to see me. She encouraged me to go to the park with her. I agreed, but I was still very scared… Scared that he would find me, scared that he would attack. I couldn't help but check over my shoulder every few seconds.

"You don't need to be afraid anymore. I can't imagine what you've been through. If you want to go back home, we can", she said.

August 2005

"No. I'm going to take the first step to living my life again. I cannot live in fear anymore. I've been afraid for too long. He can't have this over me. I have to shake this off for my own sanity".

SAY TO THOSE with fearful hearts, be strong, and do not fear, for your God is coming to destroy your enemies. He is coming to save you.
–Isaiah 35:4 NLT

CHAPTER 5

Everyone is not your FRIEND

Do not be misled: "Bad company corrupts good character." -1 Corinthians 15:33 NIV

For a while I was bestfriends with a girl named Zoey... We'd known each other since around middle school, and always spoke, but only started hanging out during our senior year. What's interesting about our relationship is that the boy, she was pregnant by my old friend Sean, and as previously stated, I messed around with Sean in the past as well.

When Zoey and I began our friendship, I was honest with her about the genesis of the relationship between Sean and I as I didn't want it to cause any discomfort. I thought that my upfront honesty was enough, but I'd later find out that it was not.

The summer after we graduated from high school, Zoey started treating me differently and acting funny. I tried not to pay them no mind and distanced myself from both of them for all of our sake. Her friendship meant too much to me for it to be ruined over a man that quite frankly didn't mean that much to me.

One day out of the blue, Zoey called me and shared that Sean had gotten someone else pregnant and in the same breath, told me that she was pregnant as well... Months later, when she had her baby, she named me the godmother, unbeknownst to me.

After giving birth, Zoey decided to move to North Philadelphia with her sister Joy and asked for my assistance. I'd met Joy not long before at the baby shower and I liked her because I thought she was goofy and always kept us laughing. We hit it off immediately, and eventually became so close that she started calling me her sister as well. Between the love I had for being around the two of them and their close proximity to my school, I began spending a lot of time with them.

We started doing everything together. One of our favorite hangout spots was a bar called Lids, where we'd go almost every Saturday night… In fact, the only time I didn't go was when I had to work the next morning, but even still, that didn't always stop me.

Over time, Zoey started dating again and was seeing a man named Chris who had a brother named Cory, who I'd eventually begin to date.

Cory had such a smart mouth. I couldn't stand him when I first met him. All we did was argue.

"I don't like you… I don't know what girls you are used to, but it's not me", I told him.

I guess he didn't feel the same way because he went behind my back and asked Zoey for my number. A few hours after we met, he called me to apologize for his behavior, and therein lies the beginning of our relationship. Cory was far from being my type, he was into the street life and was quite annoying, but I still talked to him anyway.

All the signs of him being a jerk were there, but once again, I ignored my better judgement. It didn't take long for him to become controlling. From little things to big things, he always had an opinion on what I was doing, but the one that sticks out the most was that he forbade me from going to the bar since that was his hangout spot… Ignoring his request, I decided one day that I'd go to the bar despite his wishes.

Of course, the first thing I noticed when I got there was Cory hugged up with a random girl. I walked over to him and said, "I hope you're having fun" and then I walked away. He came running behind me and asked if we could talk. He quickly hopped in the car and began arguing with me. The conversation got heated quickly and things got physical.

"Did you just slap me?" He asked.

"Yes! Didn't you put your hands on me first?"

Zoey watched everything happening from afar and walked up to the car with a brick in her hand.

"Hit her again! I dare you to hit her again!"

After that incident, I ignored Corey's calls for weeks, but eventually I got over it and decided one day that I'd accept his call against my better judgement. We talked for a while and I figured that I'd give him another chance. However, this time I made it a point to be more cautious as I felt that I couldn't trust him. I knew all along that he wasn't loyal, but I was naive as most young girls can be at times.

I had to stop hanging around Joy and Zoey as much because I was slacking on my schoolwork. Joy had started acting like she didn't want me around… When I came around, she would leave the room, wouldn't look at me, or blatantly disrespected me for no reason. But, like most things, I brushed it off.

A few weeks had passed since I last saw Zoey and Joy, and I had gone to the doctor for my physical and to get tested for an STD. I didn't think anything of it because I'd felt fine, but a few days later, I got a call from my doctor with news that said the opposite.

"Samantha you tested positive for Chlamydia and Gonorrhea", he said.

My jaw dropped. I couldn't believe what I was hearing. I tried to calm myself before I called Corey, but I couldn't. "How did this happen?!" "Two STD's?!"

Not knowing what to do, I called Winter screaming and crying about the news I'd just received.

"Samantha, HE GAVE YOU WHAT?! Call him and tell him that he needs to get tested and that you two are done. The relationship is over".

She was right.

When I got off the phone with Winter, I called Cory immediately. I didn't even give him the chance to say hello before I screamed into the phone, "Cory who else are you having sex with? Don't lie to me! I know you are cheating, so just be honest. I had the feeling you were and now I know that you just have a community penis. You couldn't wear a condom?

"Samantha, you are tripping, and I don't have time for this. I am not cheating on you", He said.

"Corey stop lying to me. I got tested and I was positive for gonorrhea"

"You have what?!"

"Oh, I'm not finished. You gave me gonorrhea and chlamydia" I exclaimed.

He asked me how was he to know that I wasn't the one who gave it to him, and I was beside myself.

"Cory do not play with me. I'm positive I didn't give it to you. I got tested before I met you. I always get tested before, during, and after my relationships. So, if you didn't cheat on me then you've been walking around with a dirty penis... You don't care? You know how scary that is? What if you had HIV/AIDS?! You should never walk around and not get tested! How could I be stupid and have unprotected sex! I know you are not that stupid and I'm not dumb so be honest... You cheated on me and didn't want to use a condom. I'm done. I've had enough of the lies and the disrespect. Don't call me ever again".

I was in the midst of hanging up the phone when he admitted to cheating, apologized for it, and confessed that he knew who he'd gotten it from.

"I don't care who it is, but you need to call and tell her to get tested. Go be with her. I hope it was worth it", and then I hung up.

A week had gone by and I hadn't heard from him at all... I noticed that my period had not come on and at this point, I was two weeks late. I figured it was because my cycle was changing. However, I wanted to be sure, so I went to Planned Parenthood and took a pregnancy test. It came out positive. I was five weeks pregnant.

I wanted to cry... I was shocked and I couldn't believe it. First it was an STD and now it's a baby? I just couldn't catch a break.

My sister was the first person I told.

"What are you going to do?" She asked.

I wasn't sure what my long-term plan would be, but I knew that I had to call Corey and tell him before I did anything else. I was so confused.

"Corey I'm only calling to tell you that I'm pregnant".

"What!?", he said in disbelief.

"I'm pregnant and I'm not sure what I want to do".

"Samantha what do you mean you don't know? You're not getting an abortion! You know it's against my religion Samantha. I know you are done, but I want you to keep it. I am going to be there for you and my child... Please don't hang up. Please don't get an abortion".

I hung up before he could even finish his sentence.

I was scared, but two days later I told my mom... She didn't say much, but I knew she was upset. She didn't talk to me for the rest of that day.

I chose not to get an abortion... A decision Cory was happy with. I knew deep down that I didn't want to be with him, but I also really did not want to be a statistic... Truthfully, I didn't know if Corey was going to be there for our child. He'd already had a daughter that he barely talked about, so how did I know he was going to be there for ours?

27

As he often would, Corey called me to check on me, and somehow, we started talking about Zoey and Joy.

"Did you tell Zoey that you were pregnant?" He asked.

"No. I haven't talked to Zoey and Joy at all. They've both been acting weird towards me lately. I've been keeping my distance.

Suddenly Corey lost his temper.

"Samantha, you know at first I did not want to talk to you because you were Zoey's friend and I did not care for her or her sister... "That's why when we first met, I was getting smart with you. You work hard and you are in school, no kids yet. You're trying to make something of yourself... That's what made me like you. I didn't want you to go to the bar every weekend because you were different. I knew you had something going for yourself".

I was shocked into silence by his submission.

"How close are you with Zoey and Joy?"

"What do you mean?"

"I know you and Zoey are best friends and you and Joy call each other sisters, but they are not your friends. You might be a friend to them, but they don't care about you. They talk about you when you're not around".

"Corey where is this coming from and how do you know if they talk about me when I'm not around?"

Corey took a deep breath.

"It's been something that I've been wanting to tell you for so long, and it's been killing me not telling you... Remember that one night you didn't go to the bar? Well, we all went to the bar and afterwards went back to Zoey and Joy house... We were all hanging out, and Joy started dancing in front of me. She grabbed me and took me into another room... Samantha, I had sex with her. They all know, but no one told you... You didn't deserve what I did to you. I am sorry I never meant to hurt you", he said.

Again, I hung up before he could say anymore.

Is this why she'd been acting funny towards me? A million things were running through my mind. A part of me wondered why he'd waited to bring it up until that moment. Was he just saying this because he doesn't like Zoe and Joy? But then again, why would he lie? Was the STD from her?

The next day when I got out of one of my classes, I texted Joy, asking her to call me when she got a chance. I knew I had to confront her.

"What's up? You wanted me to call you?", she said.

"Corey told me something about you, so I wanted to ask you rather than assume he was telling the truth", I replied.

"Samantha, who do you think you are calling me at work with this nonsense?! Don't ever call my phone again. F**k you and Corey... If I wanted him, I could have him! He's dirty anyway. Your ugly self can have him".

"All I was doing was asking you a simple question... For you to get mad and start acting like this, then it must be true. All you had to do was say no and that would've been the end of it. I called you calm... I thought we were friends... we called each other ``sister'''".

"We were never friends, you were my sisters' friend, and as for sisters, you will never be my sister and I never called you that ever... You are a hoe. I will beat you the hell up."

I started laughing

"What's funny?" she asked.

"You. I find you funny right now. You are coming at me. You must really want to fight me, knowing you can't beat me. This is getting out of hand and going too far".

"You are talking about me having sex with Corey... What about you when you had sex with Zoey baby father?! Who are you to come at me when you did the same thing to Zoey!"

I was stunned and caught off guard by the accusation.

"What? I did not have sex with Zoey baby father!" I said

"Yes, you did", she replied.

We spent some time arguing on the phone until I finally found the strength to hang up… Afterwards, I immediately called Winter.

"I called Joy to tell her what Corey told me and she went off on me, saying I'm ugly, called me ugly, dirty, a hoe, and threatened to beat me up… Oh, and get this she accused me of having sex with Zoey's baby dad.

"What?!" She responded just as stunned as I was.

I reminded her that Zoey and I were not friends when I was talking to Sean, but she already knew that. She did her best to calm me down and to reassure me, but then told me to call Zoey to settle everything, and I knew she was right.

Truthfully, I was not interested in fighting anyone, especially not over a boy, but I was also pregnant and didn't want any harm to come to my child.

I called Zoey, and we talked for a while, going back and forth for a bit… I couldn't take it for too long because I was at a loss for words and the more, she tried to justify the situation, the madder I got.

The situation with Zoey had passed as quickly as it came, and again, I decided that I was going to focus on working and saving my money since I'd had a baby on the way. I didn't want to have to depend on Corey for financial assistance or emotional support.

Around New Year's day, the reality of my situation got the best of me and I realized that my only option was to abort my child. Corey wasn't showing up the way I needed him to for anything that I deemed important and wasn't apologetic for it at all. In hindsight, I believe I made the decision to have the abortion to spite him, but I honestly think that it was the best decision for me at the time.

Corey was not too fond of the news of my abortion. He called me a murderer and damned me to Hell, and what's worse about the situation is that I agreed with him.

Lesson

I took my anger out on my pregnancy and wished that I hadn't. I didn't like the life Corey was leading, and I didn't want to bring a child into that world, but I knew that I would've had the support of my family... Because of that experience, I never allow myself to act out of anger as it never helps a situation.

FRIENDSHIP IS NOT about who you knew longer it's about who stayed and added value to your life who stick around through the bad times along with the good and help you along the way –Alisha Curry

Corresponding Scriptures

RESENTMENT KILLS A fool, and envy slays the simple –Job 5:2 NIV

HE WENT ON "what comes out of a person is what defiles them. For it is from within, out of a person's heart, that evil thoughts come- sexual immorality, theft, murder, adultery, greed, malice, deceit, lewd- ness, envy, slander, arrogance, and folly. All these evils come from inside and defile a person." –Mark 7:20-23 NIV

IN YOUR ANGER do not sin: Do not let the sun go down while you are still angry, and do not give the devil a foothold –Ephesians 4:26-28 NIV –v31 Get rid of all bitterness, rage and anger, brawling and slander, along with every form of malice.

CHAPTER 6

August 2010: The Devil's Return

No WEAPONS FORGED against you will prevail.
-Isaiah 54:17 NIV

I had just recently gotten out of a verbal abuse relationship right before I met Tristan. However, it wasn't my first time dealing with a man who was abusive. Prior to my relationship with Tristian, I dated a man named James, who would often call me names like, "whore", "hoe", "bitch", "dumb ", etc., when he got mad and all we did was argue.

James was the jealous type... If I went out with my girls, he had a problem with it.

He'd say things to me like, "What are you going out for? Only whores go out to find a man. You have one", "Why are you going out to whore around with your friends?", and, "You are going out to cheat!"... And when I would go out, he would blow my phone up, calling me non-stop, leaving erratic voice messages, countless text messages that would say, "answer your phone or it will be a problem", and I knew he would make good on his word.

There were times when I'd be at work, and he would freak out if I didn't answer his call. Eventually, it got to a point where he tried to dictate who I could and couldn't be friends with... He'd try to make me choose between him and my male best friend, Jahlil most often.

It didn't take long for me to get fed up with James' behavior, and I ended the relationship before it could get any worse.

A few months later is when I met Tristan. I had just graduated from Lincoln Tech with a degree as a Medical Assistant and was starting my externship at P-Comm. I was excited to work there, especially because my sister did as well. I didn't say it as much as I probably should've at the time, but I really appreciated her help in landing me that position.

One day after work, I had just got off the bus and was walking home when a stranger pulled over and asked me if he could talk to me for a minute. I told him that I'd oblige if he parked the car and got out to talk.

"Hi, how are you? What's your name if you don't mind me asking?" He said with a smile.

"Samantha. What is yours?"

"Tristan… Can I call you Sam for short?"

"No, I don't know you.", I said with a playful smile… At this point, I was flirting.

"You have a beautiful smile that's what made me stop to talk to you because I saw your smile".

I said thank you, even though I thought his line was corny.

"Where are you from?" He asked.

"I'm from around here… I live up the street"

"Really? I just moved on Vernon Rd… It looks like we are neighbors even though you're a block or two up from me."

We were standing four doors away from his home.

When he asked me for my phone number, I was a little skeptical because during our conversation, I found out that he was 18, and at the time, I was 21. I went back and forth with my reservations, but ultimately decided to give him a chance because he was smart, funny, cute, and I really wanted to date someone new and different.

Later that night he called me, and we talked on the phone for what felt like forever. I enjoyed talking to him, but I had a hard time getting past his age. He would call me and text me and I'd ignore him, or would never call him back, but he was very persistent.

I played around with the idea for a while until one of my work friends convinced me that I should give him a chance and just have fun. The aforementioned and then some, led me to making the phone call to him, and of course he was shocked. He invited me over to his house to watch TV and to talk that night and the rest was history.

Being with Tristan felt good. I enjoyed spending time with him, and he spoiled me... It felt good having someone who was kind and knew how to treat a woman; Someone who knew what they had and cherished it. Everything was great for a while, but it didn't last long. Four months into the relationship, everything came crashing down.

One night while we were dating, I went out with my girlfriends to a fish fry. Tristan had dropped me off and came back to pick me up. I'd had a few drinks and was a little buzzed when I got in the car, which he did not like. He wouldn't even speak to me which really hurt my feelings. I burst into tears due to the mistreatment, but he still left me, unphased. The time was 2:30 AM and I had no choice but to walk away with no set destination. His friend and my girlfriend eventually caught up with me.

"I was just upset and didn't want to be in his car... My feelings were hurt. He said he didn't want to deal with me, but I didn't even do anything".

When I got home that night, Tristan called me... I did not answer until about the fourth time.

"I'm sorry. I was upset because I know how guys take advantage of women when they are drunk.", was the first thing he said to me.

I reassured him that I knew my limit when it came to me drinking, especially when I'm out. I shared with him that I'd already had someone take advantage of me and that I wasn't going to let that happen again.

"Sam what are you saying? You were..."

"Yes. I was raped", I interjected.

35

This August will be five years since it happened... Please don't ask me any questions about it because I don't want to talk about it. I blocked it out like it didn't happen. I put it to the back of my mind".

The very next day, he came to pick me up and took me on a date to make up for what had happened the night before. We went to Arnold's Family Fun Center.

As we were driving, my phone rang out of nowhere. And when I looked to see who it was, I was surprised to see that it was James. I was racking my brain to figure out why he'd be calling me? His last words to me had been, "I hate you and you're a whore who would want you".

It didn't take long for Tristan to notice the change in my facial expression.

"Babe you ok? You want me to answer it?"

"No, you don't have to answer it, I'll let it go to voicemail"

A few weeks later Tristan, and I had a disagreement. What about? I do not know. but he wasn't answering any of my calls or texts and I began to worry... When he finally got around to calling me back, he broke up with me with no explanation and then hung up.

The next day, he came to my house unannounced... I saw him and the only thing I could say was "Tristan, what are you doing here? You already broke up with me... You wanted to do it face to face?"

"I apologize. I didn't mean it".

Something inside of me told me that it wasn't a good idea to take him back, but I did it anyway. Later that day, he came by to pick me up again. When I opened the door, he had a bouquet of roses with him. And even though his behavior had changed completely, and I felt "good" about his actions, something was telling me that I had made a mistake.

The niceness soon wore off and we began to argue again. Because both of us are very stubborn, we never talked the problem through and would end up not speaking for however long it took for one of us to put our pride aside and end the argument with an apology.

Tristian's behavior started to become concerning, so admittedly, I looked through his phone one day while using it. The first thing I found was proof that he'd been talking to another girl behind my back... And what's worse was that he'd met her on his birthday, a day that we'd spent together. The irony of all of this is that Tristian would often go through my phone because he'd assumed that I was the one cheating when really his insecurities were birthed out of his own actions. I was tired of the arguing and I was tired of the lies, but I wasn't ready to walk away just yet... We'd had some great times together and he was very attentive and caring when it was good.

My mother has always been my confidant and warned me multiple times that it was much too early for us to be arguing as much as we did. I knew deep inside that she was right, but there are some lessons that we need to learn for ourselves.

On August 15, 2010, I received yet another wakeup call. I was at Tristan's house and we'd gotten into another argument; At this point, I was over it and I was over us. The bickering had gotten to the point where I was ready to go home and the fact that I'd had a job interview the next day that I was excited about was even more incentive to leave.

In order to get away from Tristian's house without causing further strife, I secretly texted my girlfriend to call me, saying that she was on her way to see me.

When I got home, I laid across my bed and took a nap, that is until Tristan called me, waking me up.

"I thought you said you were coming back", he said.

"I never said I was... I said I'd talk to you later", I responded.

We went on and on for a while until I eventually hung up. Within a minute, he called me back, but I ignored it and attempted to fall back asleep. I was awakened once again by my phone ringing.

"Are you coming back over? I am going to take you to your interview tomorrow?"

To avoid an argument, I packed my stuff and told him to come get me.

As I was getting myself together to leave, I felt God telling me not to go, and course, I didn't listen.

F*OR IT WILL not be you speaking but the spirit of your Father speaking through you. -Matthew 10:20 NIV*

My mom stopped me as I was walking out the door.

"Where are you going... I thought you were getting ready for your interview tomorrow... Samantha, you don't need to go out. If I was you, I wouldn't go. I just have a feeling that you shouldn't go".

I thought briefly about what he said, and I knew that she was right, but before I knew it, Tristian was outside, honking his car horn. I didn't say anything to him when I got in the car because I was still mad at him... When he would talk, I would ignore him.

When we reached his father's house, I went into his room, turned on the TV and sat on the bed.

"Why did I come over here? I should've stayed home", I kept thinking to myself.

Tristan came into the room, trying to laugh and joke around but I wasn't paying him any attention.

"Why did you come over?" he asked.

"I don't know... Honestly to avoid arguing", I said.

At the time, I was so enthralled in the television and fixated on ignoring him that I didn't even notice that he'd had a gun in his hand.

He walked over to me, "playing around" because I was being stubborn, put the gun on my ankle and pulled the trigger... He didn't think it was going to go off, but it did. He shot me.

"I'm sorry. I'm sorry. I didn't mean it. I didn't think it was going to go off! I was just playing around. I'm sorry. What did I do?!"

I wanted to cry so bad, but I couldn't. The pain was unbearable. I could see the bone. I was trying to hold it together and put pressure to it to stop the bleeding before it got any worse. I yelled at him to take me to the hospital and I could see the fear in his eyes.

Tristan picked me up and carried me to car and when we got to the hospital, he carried me into the emergency room screaming for help! The staff took me back to be seen by the doctor instantly. God, it hurt so bad. They fiddled with my foot a bit until they got it wrapped up and I could no longer hold back my tears. Not just tears of pain, but also, tears of confusion. Why and how did I allow myself to get into this position? Why me?

The police came back into the room to question me about what had happened, but I was in so much pain that I didn't want to talk to them. I didn't want to talk to anyone.

"Whatever Tristan told you is true", was all that I could muster up for my story.

The doctors brought my parents back and showed them the x-rays.

"Your daughter does not have an ankle bone... The bullet shattered it, so there's nothing there. It's like a black hole. The bullet came close to hitting her main artery and she could have bled to death. She is very lucky".

While all of this was going on, the only thing I could think about was my Medical Assistant interview the next day. I had worked so hard and finally the big day was here. I asked the nurse if it would be possible for me to go and she told me that unfortunately, I'd have to stay in the hospital for a few days and that I wouldn't be able to make the interview. Again, all I could do was cry.

"How could I let this happen? Why did this happen? Why didn't I just stay in the house when I knew I should've?"

My family walked through the door not long after the nurse left, but I wanted to be strong, so I tried my best to conceal my tears.

"Sheena… I can't go to my interview tomorrow".

My sister began to sob and then left the room. My mother hugged me, and my dad cried and walked out to be with my sister as well. Eventually, they all left. And then it was just me. Alone.

The Orthopedic doctor came into the room to introduce himself and told me that I'd be having emergency surgery the next morning, the first of four.

Tristan came to see me after my procedure was complete. He sat in a chair across from my bed and had such sadness in his eyes. I could sense how bad he felt about the whole thing, but I wasn't phased by this. He tried to touch me, but I moved my hand away at every impasse. He eventually got the hint, kissed me on my forehead, and left.

My parents and my sister came back to the hospital later that morning to check on me. Once they arrived, the doctor came into the room to monitor my progress, to introduce himself, and share with them that I would have to have another surgery.

"Another surgery? When did she have the first one?", my mom said

"She had surgery this morning to see how much ankle bone was left to save and there wasn't any left to save. I cleaned the wound and placed a drainage tube there to make sure that it wouldn't get infected… For the second surgery, I will have to go in and fuse the bones together by taking bone marrow from her hip. That way she will still be able to walk. I will place a halo and screw in her foot to prevent any movement".

My sister walked in, interrupting his explanation.

He continued, "Samantha won't have any flexibility even though her bones are fused together. She will not have an ankle. The ankle is the flexible part of the bone. She won't be able to run, jump, wear heels, or move her foot around etc.".

My jaw dropped to the ground.

Will she walk normally?", my sister asked him.

"Yes. She will walk normally. She'll have a little limp for a while, but you shouldn't be able to tell when she's reached full recovery".

As promised, I had another surgery the following morning. Later that same day, my best friend Ashely paid me a visit. She sat down and looked at me when the nurse left the room and asked what happened… She insisted that I tell her the truth.

"I don't want to hear that "y'all got robbed and you got shot" story he told everyone... He did this to you didn't he?"

Deep down I knew she knew the truth and I couldn't lie to her.

I started to cry.

"Yes".

"How could you let this happen? How could he be so stupid and be playing around with a gun?", she asked.

"He didn't do it on purpose, it was an accident. It happened so fast. I didn't let it happen. I wasn't paying him any mind until it was too late", I said, defending myself and the situation.

"I hope this is it. I hope you are done with him! I'm not playing with you. Look where you are at, look at the situation you're in. A man is supposed to make you feel safe, not put you in harm's way. And tell your parents and the cops the truth... He got people thinking you were robbed, and you keep avoiding it. I know you care about him and you don't want him to go to jail, but think about yourself… If the gun was pointing somewhere else, I wouldn't be talking to you right now... You'd probably be dead!"

We both started crying… She was right.

Even though the incident changed my life forever and provided me with some new difficulties I wouldn't have otherwise had, I was thankful to be alive and for the ability to walk.

The next chance I got, I told the police what really happened that night between Tristian and I and they thanked me for my honesty. After they left, my parents came in and I told them what really happened too.

"I knew it was him because he couldn't look me in the eyes when he was talking to me", my mom said with a strong force like no other.

Her and my father were in utter disbelief.

Tristan had called me later that day and I told him that I reported the truth to everyone and that I didn't want to be with him anymore.

"Samantha, I'm sorry I really didn't mean to do this to you. I love you."

I told him that "love wouldn't have done this to me", and I hung up the phone.

I was in the hospital for two weeks on several different kinds of pain medicine and I hated the way the drugs made me feel. I had an abundance of visitors, from family, to friends, to co-workers... It kept me positive and in good spirits. I learned that nothing reveals who your true friends are better than when you're going through something.

My mother, sister and friends were there with me every step of the way; When I cried, they did too. I couldn't thank them enough for how strong they were for me. However, I wasn't particularly pleased with the way my father was handling it. He'd left me to go to North Carolina for a family reunion because he couldn't handle seeing me in such pain, but I still just couldn't understand why he'd leave me. Here I was, in the most vulnerable state I'd ever been in, in the most unimaginable pain, and yet, I felt like I wasn't his main priority.

I was released from the hospital in due time but getting back to real life proved to be difficult. The pain seemed to be getting worse and I wasn't motivated to do much of anything. I remember how hard it was for me to even go to the hairdresser. I felt like a victim and I really didn't want people to look at me that way, but with the help of my sister, I ended up going.

While I was in the hairdresser, people stared at me nonstop… One person asked me what happened, and when I didn't answer, people started to gossip right in front of my face. Was this going to be my new normal? I got stares everywhere I went.

Sheena came over to see me every day when she got off of work and my cousin would come over to keep me company while my mother was working. They'd help me bathe, get dressed, and remain positive, but I hated depending on other people and the fact that I couldn't just get up and go was unbearable. All I could see were four walls, but I still didn't want to leave.

My 22nd birthday was coming up, and my friend Kara had been so adamant about throwing me a party so I could celebrate. She decorated my house so beautifully. It was an all-black party with a splash of hot pink, and she got a cake shape of an "S" with all of my pictures on the cake… I appreciated it, but deep down, I didn't want the company because I knew that it'd be accompanied with questions and stares.

I conceded and ended up having the party and was glad I did because I had a great time being around those who loved me most, but I'd be lying if I said I secretly couldn't wait for everyone to leave. I realize now that I was trying to fight depression. I felt sorry for myself. I hated myself. I slipped deeper and deeper into a depression and became angry.

"God are you still there?"

My downward spiral worsened by the day… For a while, I stopped showering and didn't care how bad I smelled. Tristan would call to check on me often and for reasons unbeknownst to me, I would give him a little conversation. I asked the same "why" questions over and over, and he apologized profusely. But honestly, nothing that he said mattered. Every time I'd close my eyes, the events of that awful night played back in my head like a record. I thought about the bullet piercing my heart or my head; All things that would begin to haunt me.

I didn't understand why God would allow this to happen to me. I screamed. I cried. I was mad at him for not answering me. I felt that he'd turned his back on me, that he was mad at me. I had finally hit rock bottom. Seeing my friends out and about pained me in ways that are beyond comprehension. I felt even more lonely. Depression took a hold on me and nothing could cheer me up.

"I wish that bullet would have hit me elsewhere", I'd often think to myself. I wanted to die. I thought about what life would be like if I ended my life.

One night, my mother had come home from a church function at Enon Tabernacle and could see how unhappy I was. She was hurt because I was hurt… So, she took me by the hands and said, "I was at church today and I was praying for you. We were praying for you… I know you don't want to hear this, but you will get through this. It's just a little set back. God will pull you through".

She was right, I didn't want to hear about it at all.

"Here take this," she said as she handed me a piece of paper that read "Faith" and on the bottom, it read Matt 17:20.

"Because you have so little faith," He answered. "For truly I tell you, if you have faith the size of a mustard seed, you can say to this mountain, 'Move from here to there,' and it will move. Nothing will be impossible for you.'" (NIV)

After my mom read me the scripture, she grabbed my hand and started praying. I began to cry. At that moment, I knew that I had to let go of the hurt, the pain, and the anger I was harboring. I could no longer take it out on anyone, and I had to get out of the depressive state that I was in. I didn't like who I was becoming.

Later that night when I prayed to God. I made sure to hold onto my paper that contained my mustard seed and I cried again.

Through an endless flood of tears, I told him that I was mad about what had happened to me and begged for understanding. I asked him to remove the pain in my life and to restore my happiness because I couldn't take it anymore.

His response was clear and right on time.

> *"My child fear not and do not cry. I have not left you. I am here with you. I was always with you. I will never leave or forsake you. I told you not to leave the house, but you chose to ignore me and made your choice. I spoke to you and through your mother, but you still didn't hear me. My child I did save you, you are still alive, and you are still able to walk".*

My last surgery didn't happen long after God spoke to me, and I was finally starting to feel like myself again. I started being more social, taking care of myself, and attending church with my family. During one of my first services back to church, I really felt that I was receiving the word that I needed, and again, I began to cry. It felt like God was right there with me, holding me in his arms. The spirit was moving through me, and urged me to walk down the aisle to join the church... Building that relationship with God took some time, but with his help I was granted the freedom to release the pain and hurt I was so badly suffering from.

GOD HURTS, BUT *he also bandages up; he injures, but his hands also heal. Even seven troubles will not harm you. ~Job 5:18-19 NCV.*

Reflection

Have you ever been angry at God? Have you ever blamed God for the things you have encountered? Have you asked God, where was he? Why didn't he intervene? Why didn't he show up? Why me? Well, that was me.

I was angry as a child. I was angry as a teen. And I was angry for the majority of my twenties.

Red was the fire that burned in me from the pain that I'd endured. The forced smiles I had to give people to make them believe I was okay, the horrifying truth I hid to protect others, the picture-perfect life I created when deep down I felt that I wasn't good enough, pretty enough, or smart enough.

I've endured troubles, letting people take advantage of me, not having respect for my body, being raped, being shot, encountering unhealthy relationships, and experiencing other traumas that I'm still working through.

Lessons

Life often brings you matters that are difficult to swallow, like an illness, unemployment, the death of a loved one, etc., but, rest assured, God has something good planned for your life, even if you can't see it. He is actively working to bring the best out of you in every situation and to encourage you to hold onto hope in the midst of tough times. In the midst of struggle, you will need to grab a hold of this truth.

The Bible says, "We know that God causes everything to work together for the good of those who love God and are called according to his purpose for them" (Romans 8:28 NLT)… It isn't saying that every day will be a good one, we know that that isn't true, but what it does say is that when you put your whole life together, every piece of it works together for your good. It's kind of like making a cake… You may not like the taste of each ingredient individually, but when it's all put together, you can't keep your hands off of it. God wants to bake your life, even if it means that he has to use some ingredients that taste awful on their own.

God does not promise that everything will work out the way we want it to or that every story will have a happy ending… Not every business decision will make you a million dollars, not every couple that gets married will live happily ever after, not every child will become captain of their sports team… Instead, the verse reminds us that we ought to confidently relinquish control to the Master and deal with the hand we're dealt. He will never put more on us than we can bear.

Hope isn't the same as optimism. It isn't the belief that something bad will turn out well. It's the absolute confidence that every part of your life ultimately makes sense regardless.

From our vantage point, life sometimes looks like a mess, but God's view from Heaven isn't the same as ours.

Finally, be strong in the Lord and in his great power. Put on the full armor of God so that you can fight against the devil's evil tricks.

You can't even imagine the good that God has in store for you… In Jeremiah 29:11, he says, "I have good plans for you, not plans to hurt you. I will give you hope and a good future"

Your future is in God's hands — and there's no better place for it to be.

~ Tamara Callands

Coinciding Scriptures

CAST ALL YOUR anxiety on him because he cares for you.
-1Peter 5:7 (NIV)

SO DO NOT fear, for I am with you; do not be dismayed, for I am your God. I will strengthen you and help you; I will uphold you with my righteous hand. –Isaiah 41:10 (NIV)

HEALING TAKES TIME. The Lord is near to the brokenhearted and saves those who are crushed in spirit. –Psalm 34:18 (KJV)

GUIDE ME IN your truth and teach me, for you are God my savior, and my hope is in you all day long. -Psalm 25:5 (NCV)

GOD IS MY salvation; I will trust Him and not be afraid. The Lord, himself is my strength and my defense; he has become my salvation. -Isaiah 12:2

FROM THE END of the earth I call to you, I call as my heart grows faint; lead me to the rock that is higher than I, for you have been my refuge in the shelter of your wing. -Psalm 61:2-2 NIV

AND WE ALL, who with unveiled faces contemplate the Lord's glory, are being transformed into his image with ever increasing glory, which comes from the Lord who is the spirit. -Corinthians 3:18 (NIV)

MY CHILD THIS is not for you to understand just yet, but you will trust me and have faith hold onto your mustard seed and don't lose faith. -Ephesians 6:10-11 (NCV)

WE KNOW THAT God causes everything to work together for the good of those who love God and are called according to his purpose for them.-Romans 8:28 (NLT)

DON'T BE AFRAID, for I am with you. Don't be discourage, for I am your God. I will strengthen you and help you. I will hold you up with victorious right hand – Isaiah 41:10 (NLT)

CHAPTER 7

Actions Over Words

IN A WORLD filled with noise find your voice by speaking to God.
—Samantha Williams

I thought my poor track record with men was over, but that was only until I met Liam; My bad habit that I couldn't shake. We first met while I worked at Allegheny Valley School, (AVS), but our relationship continued beyond that. When I first saw him, I thought he was different... I was attracted to his dimples and thought he'd had a really cute smile.

He noticed me one day after exiting the elevator and asked for my name.

"My name is Samantha, and yours?", I said politely.

"Liam... I know you are new working here. I've never seen you before"

The conversation we had was short and after that, I didn't see him for a few days, but that didn't stop me from asking around about him.

When I finally did see Liam again, I grabbed his arm and told him to come here.

He laughed.

"What's funny?" I asked.

"You are grabbing my arm, telling me to get over here", he said with a smirk.

We started talking and walked outside, and by the end of the conversation, we'd exchanged numbers. From then on, we started texting and hanging out, but I figured we were just friendly. I'd heard that Liam was known for being a big flirt at work and that he had already talked to a few girls at the job, but I don't listen to hearsay and I knew I didn't want anything serious with him anyway.

A couple of days had gone by and I received a message from him stating that he didn't want to talk anymore because he wasn't emotionally attracted to me and that he felt there was nothing between us except some sexual tension.

I reread the message countless times. "Did I miss something?", I asked myself. He hadn't even given me a chance, and it hurt even more because I did end up catching feelings for him even though that wasn't my initial intention.

I asked if we could talk more in person about it and he said, "ok".

The next day when I got to work, I pulled Liam aside and asked if we could talk.

"What do you want to talk about?", he said.

"Your text. I felt like you weren't being honest... If you talk to somebody or have a girl, just say that, don't give me some dumb excuse or lie by saying that you don't feel anything for me... If you don't want to be serious, that's fine... It's not like we can't be friends".

"No. I don't talk to anybody. I am telling you the truth. I don't see myself taking you seriously or getting emotionally attracted and I don't want to waste your time, but you're right just because I don't see you that way, don't mean we can't be friends."

I knew he was lying, but I went on my way, fully accepting that our relationship would be nothing more than cordial.

A few days later, a girl I didn't know approached me and asked if I had been seeing Liam because she was best friends with the girl that he was seeing.

"Why are you asking me and not him?", I said.

"Liam is a liar. You never get the truth from him, so I figured I would ask you instead. See you are new here and you don't know him... He sees you as fresh meat since everyone else here already knows how he is."

I wondered why she was the one to ask me about Liam instead of the girl he was supposedly seeing and then I put it together that maybe she was the one that was dating him.

Days had gone by since that encounter and I was over the situation, after all, I barely knew him. However, I did see him and that girl a few days later hugged up in a corner. I guess my hunch was correct.

The extent of Liam's and my communication with each other was "hi" and "bye" when we'd see each other in passing, but only if he wasn't with his girl. I eventually grew tired of him blatantly disregarding me when his girlfriend was around, so I confronted him about it.

"Liam listen we need to talk. I'm not fake, so I am going to treat you like how I treat females... if we are supposed to be cool then you shouldn't pick and choose when you want to speak to me. I don't do the fake stuff. I get that you're trying to respect your girl's feelings, but honestly, she shouldn't care if you say hi. Me and you were never together.... Anyway, I'd rather you not speak to me ever if you can't speak when she is around".

"You are right. From now on, I will speak even when she is next to me."

After that conversation, he started speaking to me and texting me again... I honestly think it's because he noticed that another man was interested in me too. Him and his girlfriend had broken up so our communication got more frequent and I thought we were really starting to connect until he randomly became distant and blocked me from contacting him.

An entire week had gone by before he called me, acting as if nothing ever happened. I didn't want to be friends and I didn't want to put my time and energy into him again. I was seeing somebody new and I had an inkling that he was seeing his ex-again as well. But even still, this was far from the end of our story.

My Sister had a cookout for 4th of July and I invited my best friend Lish and Liam as well. Her block was packed with people and my sister's neighbor was selling water ice with alcohol in it, which always makes for an interesting time. I think I'd had about two or three cups prior to Liam's arrival, and when I finally saw him, I was shocked that he really came... We sat on the steps, laughing and talking, and before I knew it, the party was over, but I still wasn't ready to go, and neither was Liam.... He and I stayed behind and talked for a while before he drove me home; Talking led to kissing and then kissing led to sex.

"We should stop... This is wrong", I said. I put my clothes on and scurried into the house without hesitation.

After that, Liam became very consistent with calling, texting, and coming to see me. All of the attention seemed like a turn in the right direction, so I ended up giving him another chance. However, as soon as things got serious between the two of us, he started going M.I.A again. There were times where I wouldn't hear from him for two weeks. I was over it. I just couldn't understand why he would beg and plead for another chance and then do the same thing again.

I decided that I was going to teach him a lesson. Everytime he texted me, I would reply with one word, two hours later, and then sometimes, I just wouldn't respond at all. He didn't like that, but it was what he deserved.

Out of curiosity, I decided to snoop, and I landed on the Instagram page of his child's mother, only to find out that he was still seeing her. I knew it was time for me to leave him alone.

Liam had called me a few days later, but I never said anything about the photo or the fact that he'd been completely M.I.A for the last few weeks. And I didn't need to bring it up either because he could sense that something had changed between us. He couldn't stand just being my friend and tried everything he could to change that. I was so sure that his smooth talking wasn't going to work this time, but he had already become a bad habit that I couldn't break.

It didn't take long for me to realize that he was only consistent when he was in the friendzone and finally, I'd had enough. I wasn't stupid and I knew something wasn't right... Lish had come over and we were having a girl's day, (dinner and a movie). Liam was calling me all night, and finally texted me after he realized that I wasn't going to answer.

"I'm on a date", I messaged back.

He was mad, and I knew how he'd take that message, but technically, I wasn't lying.

Lish and I went to the movies after we ate and then called it a night. I ended up calling Liam almost as soon as I got in the house.

"Why are you mad... You have no reason to be mad. We're not together... We are just friends".

"Samantha, I don't care. You know how I feel about you. I don't want to be your friend and I don't want to hear you say that you are out on a date with another guy."

I laughed and told him that I had gone out with Lish, not a man, and he hung up.

The next day, I decided I was going to reach out to him, but he'd blocked me. Even as friends he'd pull that same old disappearing act and I was fed up. I guess I was wrong. We couldn't even be friends.

With all the uncertainty surrounding Liam and his whereabouts, I figured I should get tested for HIV/AIDS and other STI's. I made it a point to get tested frequently regardless, but something in me told me that I needed to make an appointment asap.

A couple days after my appointment, my doctor called and told me that my test had come up positive for Chlamydia. I was furious, especially because he probably knew that he'd given it to me and still didn't say anything.

I called Lish crying as soon as I found out.

"I think I know why Liam did a disappearing act this time... Remember a couple of days ago I went to the doctor's? Well my doctor called and told me I had chlamydia and I think he knew he had it and gave it to me... Nothing he does surprises me", I said.

"You really think that's the reason?", she asked.

In that moment, I thought back to a moment of weakness I'd recently had contacted when I was over Nasir and we ended up having oral sex... I needed to let him know that he should get tested as soon as possible. Another mess.

"Do you not know your worth? Do you feel like you have to give your body away that you have to have sex to keep a man? Do you feel like you're not worth anything? You don't have to have sex with every guy you talk to you are worth so much more!" Lish said.

I felt so judged at that moment. I knew that she'd only said what she said because she cared about me, but that didn't make it any less difficult to hear. And I suppose it hurt as much as it did because I knew I felt the same way.

Was I having sex just to have it? After getting raped and not really having someone to confide in about how it'd affected, I just did it without fear of repercussions. It seemed as if no had lost its' meaning, so I gave into it because I thought that empowered me. But the more I thought about it, the more I understood that I truly did deserve much more than sex.

A month later, during a phone conversation with Lish, I received an unexpected text from Liam.

"Hey. How are you? I miss you... Was just wondering how you were doing."

Lish and I got off the phone and I couldn't help but stare at the text... Did he really just text me as if he didn't give me chlamydia and walked away without saying anything? I was boiling on the inside, but I couldn't stop reading his text. I knew I shouldn't respond, but I did.

"Are you kidding me? How am I doing? Why do you care? Didn't you disappear? I have no words for you... I'm done. And the fact that you had Chlamydia and knew you had it and didn't say anything to me is crazy. I lost all respect for you", I yelled into the phone as if it was his face.

"I didn't know I had it, but when I got tested, it was after I left, and I didn't think to call or text you to say go get tested and for that I am sorry. I should have said something... But I didn't think you would want to hear from me after doing another disappearing act on you. I knew you were mad, and I didn't want you to hate me if I called telling you to get tested after I disappeared".

"How does that sound? You are selfish and you only think about yourself! Yes, you're right, I was mad and didn't want to hear from you AT ALL. But I'm sure that you only got tested because someone told you too, and the fact you knew and never said anything to me is crazy. I won't forgive you. Luckily, I always get tested... You had me thinking you walked away because you gave me an STI, but to find out you walked away before you found out about the STI, and this time we were just friends... How about you do what you do best and disappear... And this time, stay gone".

Liam didn't listen. He kept calling and texting me, asking for another chance. I put him on the block list but took him right back off. I ignored him for a while, but again, I decided that I would give him a chance to at least be a good friend again. It took me a while to figure out why I continued to be naive, but I understand now that I was in love with him and I lacked love for myself. He'd tried so hard to be with me as he always did, but I didn't want to open myself up to him again.

Eventually, I let my guard down and I allowed him to reenter my space. I still had a wall built up, but I could tell that he was really trying. I enjoyed being around him because we were friends, but I was so naive.

55

Every Wednesday we'd go on a date and would take turns picking out a place and treating. It didn't last long though. He started canceling our dates and when he did show up, he'd be really late. For example, If he was supposed to pick me up at 8 pm, he wouldn't come until 10 pm-10:30 pm. I knew I was not his priority and he showed me that time and time again.

A few weeks later, we were talking on Facetime and he dropped a bomb on me that he and the mother of his child, Ka'maya, were going away on vacation together. His reasoning was that Ka'maya's mother was getting married in the Dominican Republic and that they wanted him to walk his daughter down the aisle, but something about that didn't feel right to me. And, it's safe to say that the rest of the conversation did not go well.

Following our phone conversation, I was upset, and it was apparent. I didn't want to talk to anyone or be bothered, but when I got to work, my friend Kylie prodded as to why I looked so upset. My eyes got watery all of a sudden, and I told her all about what had happened with Liam.

Hours had gone by since I told Kylie and it was time for me to go home. I got myself together, and I called Liam to tell him once again that the relationship was over. We argued a bit and then I hung up because there was nothing else to talk about. He tried calling back, but I ignored it. I was done.

My eyes filled with tears at the thought of all that had just transpired. He clearly didn't care about me, he didn't respect me, and he didn't even fight for it. Why was I allowing someone I treated so good to give me nothing in return? Had I learned nothing from my past?

Coinciding Scriptures

ABOVE ALL ELSE, guard your heart, for everything you do flows from it. –Proverbs 4:23 (NIV)

THERE IS A time for everything and a season for every activity under the heavens. -

ECCLESIASTES 3:1 (NIV)

TUNE YOUR EARS to wisdom and concentrate on under-standing. Cry out for insight and ask for understanding. ~Proverbs 2:2-3 (NLT)

FOR THE LORD grants wisdom! From this mouth comes knowledge and understanding. He grants a treasure of common sense to the honest. He is a shield to those who walk with integrity. He guards the path of the just and protects those who are faithful to HIM. Then you will understand what is right, just, and fair, and you will find the right way to go. For wisdom will enter your heart, and knowledge will fill you with Joy. Wise choices will watch over you. Understanding will keep you safe.–Proverbs 2:6-11 (NLT)

CHAPTER 8

The Mask

KNOW YOURSELF WORTH and respect yourself if you don't then who will? ~Alisha Curry

I was dating the same type of men, but I see now that they were just the devil himself, showing up in different masks... I didn't recognize the pattern until I met Monte. After all that I'd been through, you'd think that I would've learned my lessons, but I didn't. The signs were always right there in front of me, but I'd always had these blinders on that'd allow me to ignore the signs until the situation got way too out of hand.

Monte and I met at a breakfast store called Roxie.

"Good morning, beautiful", he called after me.

We chatted a bit, learned a little more about each other, exchanged numbers, and made plans to see each other in the near future... The next morning, I woke up to a text from him, asking if we could get dinner soon.

As always, I second guessed my decision because I wasn't sure if I was ready to engage in something new, but ultimately, I said yes. We went on our first date on a Saturday evening.

That night, I learned a lot about Monte, including the fact that he had four kids with 3 different women, and he lived with one of them still, and that he had a bad temper. He was far from my type and the signs were all there, but I ignored them.

Monte asked me to be his girlfriend a few weeks later, and I said yes, even though deep down I knew it was a bad idea. Aside from him immediately telling me who and how he was, I felt like we were moving a little too fast. As always, I ignored how I truly felt inside, but it didn't take him long to show me his dark side. He was right; Monte was unapologetically disrespectful, rude, immature, accusatory, and very verbally abusive.

The more our partnership progressed, the more I disliked him. I wanted out of the relationship. The good times we had were few and far in between. All we did was argue. I recall one time that we were in the car, joking and playing around. I said something smart, and he choked me so hard I couldn't breathe. He'd blacked out and I could see the rage in his eyes.

"See I told you to stop playing with your smart mouth. I didn't even really choke you", he said.

This sort of behavior continued for the duration of our relationship. He was no stranger to completing and threatening violent acts, both towards me and any guy who even dared to look my way. At one point, it got so bad that I prayed my phone wouldn't ring around him because I feared what he would do if he saw another man texting or calling me... I had once again reached my breaking point. I knew I should have been done with Monte, and I honestly don't know why I stayed with him only to be treated poorly. But if I had to guess, I probably stayed because I was trying to fill the void in my life that Liam had left.

There are an abundance of examples of the poor treatment I faced at the hands of Monte, but this was one of the worst... I had been at work, not paying attention to my phone, and I'd noticed that Monte called. It had been 15-20 minutes since he'd called and I knew if I called him back, it'd be a fight about how I didn't call him right back. He wasn't used to me not being at his beck and call.

I decided to call him back on my break and the first thing he said to me was, "you are being sneaky, doing something you don't have any business doing".

My explanation that I was busy at work wasn't enough for him and so an argument ensued. I was inching further and further down to the end of my rope, so I decided to end the relationship right before I ended the call. That night, he sent me insentient calls and disrespectful texts until I finally decided to answer.

"So, you really done with me? You know I love you. I didn't mean anything I said, I was just mad because you weren't answering your phone", he said. But it didn't matter. I was done.

Shortly after, Monte began sending me threatening texts, stating that he wanted the money that he'd spent on me back and that if he didn't get it, he'd bust the windows out my car, and I knew he was serious.

"I want my money back. I'm not going to leave you alone until I get all my money back that I spent on you. I wasted my time and my money on you, and I want it back. You ugly, broke, your breath stinks, you're a bitch, good for nothing and I wished I never met you", he said.

I made it a point to remain calm and not to disrespect him as I was reading his texts.

My mother came into the room and noticed that something was wrong with me. I told her that I'd ended the relationship with Monte and to my surprise, both her and my father were thrilled at the news. Unbeknownst to me, neither of them liked him to begin with, and my dad, who doesn't say much about anyone that I date, felt that there was something "off" about him.

"He keeps sending me threatening texts saying he going to bust the window out my car if he doesn't get his money back", I told my mom.

"What money?", she asked.

"The money that he spent on me when we went out to eat a few times and when he gave me money to get my nails done… That's about it".

"Samantha are you kidding me? He is not a man. NO MAN, and I mean no man, asks for his money back…Okay, so he took you out to eat and got your nails done. What is that? It's NOTHING for him to say that he is going to bust the windows out over a couple of dollars. It's not like he spent any real money on you. He is not going to touch your car. He wants his money. I'll give it to him so that he can leave you alone".

My mom left the room and went into her bedroom to tell my dad what was going on, and all I could hear was my dad saying, "you not giving him no money, and he is not going to touch Samantha's car either! Who does he think he is? He's not going to threaten my child. Where is Samantha? Call him and let me talk to him… Let me tell him straight."

Monte ended up calling me before my dad could call him.

"You got my money?", he yelled.

"Hold on. My dad wants to speak to you".

"I don't want to speak to your dad, who he thinks he is? I will bust the window out of your dad's car too if I don't like how he's talking to me."

I passed my dad the phone with no hesitation.

Monte and my dad went back and forth for what felt like forever… About the money, about what it means to be a real man, how subpar Monte thought my sex was, and that I gave him an STD, which was not at all true, in fact, it was the other way around. I was so embarrassed. How could he lie like that?

I have no idea how the conversation escalated so quickly, but by the end of the call he was talking about rounding up girls to come to my house to jump me and then mentioned he had a gun too for my dad. "You going to shoot me? "Call the cops!", my mom screamed.

She talked to the police briefly and they took my statement, but ultimately couldn't do anything except advise me to get a restraining order against Monte.

The next morning, I went downtown with my sister and my dad to get the restraining order on Monte, and the whole time, I couldn't help questioning why I stayed in the relationship for so long. The signs were there from the beginning and he told me who and how he was. But once again, I settled, and once again, I learned my lesson.

After everything with Monte, I felt like I needed a fresh start… A new beginning. There was nothing in Philly holding me back and I needed a change. That change would be Atlanta, Georgia.

My move to Atlanta was my first real step out on faith. God was leading me there and it wasn't my job to question it. I began to fully understand that he would never lead me astray. However, the closer I got to move-in day, the more I questioned whether God was orchestrating the move or if I was just subconsciously running away from my problems.

Lesson

If a man disrespects you, exit stage left because he won't change. If he shows you early on who he is, walk away. Don't settle for disrespect. It's not worth it. Love yourself more.

Coinciding Scriptures

THE LORD IS close to the brokenhearted and saves those who are crushed in spirit. ~Psalm 34:18 (NIV) He will cover you with his feathers, and under his wings you will find refuge; his faithfulness will be your shield and rampart. ~Psalm 91:4

*N*EVER PAY BACK *evil with more evil. Do things in such a way that everyone can see you are honorable. Do all that you can to live in peace with everyone. Dear friends, never take revenge. Leave that to the righteous anger of God. For the scriptures say, "I will take revenge; I will pay them back," says the Lord. ~Romans 12:17-19 NLT*

*F*AITH MAKES ALL *things possible. For nothing is impossible with God. ~Luke 1:37 NLT*

*T*O YOU, *L*ORD, *I call; you are my rock, do not turn a deaf ear to me. For if you remain silent, I will be like those who go down to the pit. Hear my cry for mercy as I call to you for help, as I lift up my words towards your Most Holy Place. ~Psalm 28:1-2 (NIV)*

CHAPTER 9

The End of an Era

I felt that there was nothing else left for me in Philly after all that had happened; All the pain and all the heartache. I wanted to escape it. Once my mind was made up to move, I called my favorite cousin, Megan, to ask if I could stay with her in Atlanta, and thankfully, she said yes. She was so excited to have me, which felt good because it was the first time in a while that I'd really felt wanted. I gave myself three weeks to move to Atlanta.

One day, not long before I left, I got a random text from Liam saying that he'd realized that I was the one he wanted to be with and begged for me to give him another chance. Of course, I was apprehensive, but his words felt sincere… He was heartbroken when I told him I was moving to Atlanta. So, me being me, I decided that I was going to give him a chance to prove himself once again before I left. Everything was great until he revealed to me that he was still living with his child's mother. He tried to explain the situation to me, promising that it was platonic and that he was doing her a favor by living with her, but his past led me to question everything he said.

Liam and I started to talk again, but I had my doubts and always felt like he was lying. To remedy this, I figured it was best to take things slow between us, and to my surprise, it worked. Things were actually going really well between us. I was surprised at how consistent he was being because his history was the exact opposite, but he impressed me. He was finally proving that he was ready to take us seriously.

We talked often about my upcoming move to Atlanta and how badly he wished I wouldn't go. I knew the time apart would be hard, but he promised to come visit and I said I'd do the same.

A week prior to my departure, Liam asked me to come over to his house and spend the day with him–I told him I would think about it. A part of me was telling me not to go. I kept having this feeling about him, but I couldn't explain why. I just knew that something didn't feel right. Liam called me and asked was I still coming over to spend the day with him and I said "no" ... I knew he was only inviting me because his child's mother was out of town with their daughter.

The fact that I was leaving for Atlanta in a few days was enough to convince me that I should go see Liam like he wanted. We spent the day watching TV, cooking, and talking about how we met and that letting me go was a huge mistake. He said that he knew that he should've chosen me and genuinely believed that we were destined to be together. And even after us having such a great day together, I was still apprehensive.

"Do you really think we can make this long-distance thing work? It's hard enough for me to see you now and you're only 15 minutes away", I said to him.

"We can just be friends. I don't want to start something with you and then leave".

"Samantha we can make anything work. I love you and I want to be with you. Now that I have you back in my life, I am not letting you go. I'm not trying to lose you at all. I mean, I am losing you because you're moving down south to Atlanta, but I don't want to lose you to another guy. I do wish I came back into the picture before you made this decision because I feel like that wouldn't have even been a thought." he responded.

His commitment to us took me aback and was very refreshing compared to how our conversations usually went. I couldn't stop thinking about if the relationship would really be different this time and if his change was permanent. The thoughts lingered in my mind even after I left his house, but deep down, the answer seemed to be "no".

That night, when I got home, I had to finish packing. There was so much that needed to get done in such little time. I planned to have a going away dinner and one last night out with my friends who couldn't make it. The closer I got to moving day, the more anxious, overwhelmed, and unsure I became; however, I knew that I had to leave Philly. Subconsciously, I wanted Liam to ask me to stay and to fight for our relationship, but in hindsight, I knew all along that he wouldn't.

Moving day was approaching quickly, and Liam hadn't mentioned any special plans for us before I left because he didn't have any. He'd promised me that he would see me later that night before I left, but I knew he was lying.

Terrell and I had a really striking conversation that same evening about Liam, and his words rang like a bell in my ears.

"Sam, you know Liam said that you two were together and he said that he was your boyfriend?"

Shocked, I responded "He did? I'm shocked because we didn't talk about that. I told him I didn't want to be in a relationship with him because I was leaving... I don't know, I asked him if he could handle a long-distance relationship".

"Do you trust him?", my brother asked.

"He is showing me that he's changed so far, he is okay".

"But do you trust him?"

I wasn't sure why he was pushing the matter so hard.

"Sam, he is going to be living a double life. He has his baby mom here and you're his girl, there , in another state. That's a win for him… When he needs to get away, he can come see you, and when he's home he's got his baby mom"

I replayed the conversation back in my head.

"Could he be right?", I wondered.

But then I remembered what Lish said, "Until he proves you wrong… So far, he is showing you that he changed and is not playing any more games, and he is being honest with you. He told you that the mother of his child lives with him when he didn't have to".

Remembering that Lish didn't like Liam at first, the fact that she grew to accept him made me think that maybe my brother was being paranoid and overprotective.

Liam finally ended up coming by to see me for a brief moment right before I hit the road at 12 am… "Sam, I am going to miss you", was the last thing he said to me that night.

Coinciding Scriptures

THE LORD IS my light and my salvation; I will fear no one. The LORD protects me from all danger; I will never be afraid. When evil people attack me and try to kill me, they stumble and fall. Even if a whole army surrounds me, I will not be afraid; even if enemies attack me, I will trust God. I have asked the LORD for one thing; one thing only do I want: to live in the Lord's house all my life, to marvel there at his goodness, and to ask for guidance. In times of trouble he will shelter me; he will keep safe in his Temple and make me secure on a high rock. So I will triumph over my enemies around me with shouts of joy. I will offer sacrifices in his Temple; I will sing; I will praise the LORD. Hear me, LORD, when I call to you! Be merciful and answer me! When you said, "come worship me," I answered, I will come, LORD. Don't be angry with me; don't turn your servant away. You have been my help; don't leave me, don't abandon me, O God, my savior. My father and mother may abandon me but the LORD will take care of me. Teach me, LORD, what you want me to do and lead me along a safe path because I have many enemies. Don't abandon me to my enemies, who attack me with lies and threats. I know that I will live to see the LORD goodness in this present life. Trust in the LORD. Have faith, do not despair. Trust in the LORD. ~Psalms 27:1-14 GNT

CHAPTER 10

The Beginning and the End

When my dad and I arrived in Atlanta, I could not believe that I really made the move. Surprisingly, it hadn't hit me yet that I was not going back to Philadelphia, and that Atlanta was my new home. My first few weeks in Atlanta, I'd be staying with my cousin Megan until I could land on my feet with a job and an apartment.

Megan and her son, Jamir, were so welcoming and as excited to see me as I was them.

"Has it hit you yet that you are here…living here?", she asked me.

"No!"

Megan set up her basement really nice for me, and I couldn't have been more appreciative. She brought a new bed for me, and she also bought paint so that I could make the room my own.

We dropped my dad off at the airport the next morning to go back home, and that's when it finally hit me. The thought of him leaving me there made my eyes water a bit, but I couldn't cry. This was what I wanted, and it was time for me to grow up.

I thought that my move to Atlanta would be a good fresh start, but drama and trials have a way of following you no matter where you go if you don't handle your problems upfront. When I moved to Atlanta, Megan was one of my favorite cousins, and I really loved her, but it didn't take long for her to show me her other side.

When I first got to ATL, I was beyond excited. I loved being there and had extremely fond memories of the times I'd spent there prior to my move. I just knew that it would be nothing but fun once I found a job. However, my job search process became exhausting and overwhelming after a while, and I hated depending on others to help pay my bills until I could afford to myself. I really loved staying with Megan at first, but my mom always told me to never overstay my welcome anywhere, so I knew that the time I'd be staying there was temporary, even though Megan told me there was no rush to leave.

"Sam, just stay here with me and save your money rather than getting your own place. That way if you decide to get your own place here or back in Philly, you'll have the money", she would often say to me.

The stress of finding a concrete job started to get to me; I was beginning to get a little homesick, and I really missed Liam even though we talked every day. I hadn't been in Atlanta for a month yet, and he'd already made plans to come visit me. I was so excited that he was coming. Megan too seemed really excited to finally meet Liam when I told her about his visit. She promised to give me my privacy and to stay out of our way the weekend that he was coming.

A month later, he fulfilled his promise and came to visit me. I was so excited to see him that I ran up to give him a hug when I saw him. I couldn't stop smiling. The days that we spent together were the best... Going out to eat, showing him all around Atlanta, hanging out, and cuddling. In fact, we had such a great time that I cried on our last day together. Partially because he was leaving, but also because I knew that there was a good chance that he was still hiding something from me. Even though we had a great time together, I couldn't help but feel like he wasn't fully himself when he was with me, almost like his mind wasn't 100% there sometimes.

I slipped into a depression about a week after Liam left. The second month of me being in Atlanta was the horizon and I still hadn't found a job. And to make matters worse, Liam had blocked me again for whatever reason, so I wasn't even able to vent to him. All I could think was, here we go again.

My mind immediately went back to the conversation that I'd had with my brother before I left. He must've been right about Liam all along. Out of curiosity, I went on Instagram and looked at Ka'maya's page. The first thing I saw was a photo of the two of them on FaceTime, making silly faces at each other... I screenshot the photo and sent it to him with the intent of seeing what lie he'd come up with to save himself. I was wondering if my text was going to through due to, he had me on the block list.

"Ka'maya posted it but she deleted it, and she's sorry she didn't mean no disrespect, knowing that we are together".

Lies.

These games he was playing hurt even worse because I was already feeling depressed and homesick, and the person that I wanted to talk to the most was nowhere to be found. How could I want to be with someone who couldn't even be there for me?

I went back on Ka'maya page and was looking at her pictures. If her and Liam were broken up as he said, why did she still have photos of just the two of them on her page? The picture that stood out the most was one with them on the couch, wearing nothing but their underwear and t-shirt.

Every morning, the first thing I'd do was put my phone on do-not-disturb (DND) because I didn't want to be bothered by anyone at all. I binge watched Grey's Anatomy on Netflix, and there were a few times where I found myself crying... My depression was getting worse. I didn't have a job, I was lonely, and I felt nothing like myself.

Megan began to notice my downslide and her concern was palpable. She'd constantly ask me what was wrong and then try to do her best to console me and reassure me that she was always going to be there for me when I needed a shoulder.

The first step of my healing was getting rid of all memories I had of Liam. He'd given me two sweatshirts and a necklace plus I had a few pictures that we took together, and I decided to place them on the grill, and burn them. I watched as the items went ablaze. And I even started to feel better... so much so that I recorded it.

A week had gone by since my Angela Bassett, *Waiting to Exhale* moment, and I was still ignoring Liam's calls. His excuse for going M.I.A this time was that he and Ka'maya had been arguing about the time he'd spent with me, even though he claims she knew we were together. He also said that he was going through a lot and didn't know how to handle it—I didn't believe his reasoning for a second. However, after he revealed that his mother had recently suffered a heart attack, I felt guilty for questioning him, so again, I gave him a pass.

Megan overheard us on Facetime and immediately got irritated by the sound of his voice. After we hung up, she asked if I was talking to him again.

"Yes", I responded, feeling a bit ashamed. I explained to her the reasoning behind why he'd suddenly become so distant, but she didn't find it plausible.

"... Hopefully he is telling the truth. I don't believe him, but if it's true then that's my bad... Just be careful with him. I am telling you what I know. Something is not right with him."

I started working two new jobs; One at Walmart Neighborhood Market and the other, Comcast... On my last day of training at Comcast, I noticed that I'd had three missed calls from a blocked number. I wondered who it could've been because I'd just changed my number because someone posted my phone number on Craigslist as a joke. The blocked caller called me once more, but this time I decided to answer. And as soon as I picked up the phone, the person on the other end hung up. I quickly put two and two together and realized that it was Ka'maya.

Between the drama that came with Liam, my new busy work schedule, and my deteriorating relationship with Megan, I couldn't catch a break.

Suddenly, Megan began to treat me differently. When she would cook dinner, instead of making enough for the three of us as she'd been doing, she would only make enough for her and her son. I'd come home from work hungry, asking if there were any leftovers and she would either tell me "no" or say that she'd only made enough for her and her son.

The dynamic changed completely, especially after our cousin Zoey and her daughter got evicted from their apartment and were forced to move in with us as well.

Arguments started to ensue over trivial things, like a ticket I'd gotten a month prior for driving in the HOV lane.

"I swear you live in your own little world. You think you know it all and you don't. Didn't I tell you? Didn't I tell you? I told you that you live in your own little world. You are not grown, and you have no idea what goes on outside your world"

I was shocked at the way she was talking to me as if I was a child. Where was this coming from? Instead of arguing back, I bit my tongue and left out for work.

For the next few days after our confrontation, I kept to myself. We'd both been avoiding each other so we hadn't seen each other at all. I had nothing to say to her and she had nothing to say to me. A week later, she sent me a message, stating that she was moving in March, which was only a few weeks away.

"Are you going to get your own place, move back home, or stay with me? If you are going to stay with me, I am going to charge you rent", the message read.

My first thoughts were how am I going to get my own place when I just started working in November? And why was she suddenly now going to charge me rent? Something was off.

I responded to her, asking her when exactly she was moving.

"March 22", she responded.

I was baffled; Baffled that she was suddenly moving and baffled at the fact that we were having the conversation through text. But that's when it hit me... She had been telling me to save my money up because she was always planning to start charging me rent eventually.

Upset, I called my mom to inform her of the shenanigans that were going on.

"Samantha, why would she have you come stay with her if she was going to move? And now, she wants you to pay her rent? That is ridiculous. This is why I didn't want you to move there unless you had your own place and enough money saved up. Samantha, come back home. I had the feeling Megan was going to do something like this", she told me.

Ever since that conversation where Megan told me that she was moving, we began to bump heads. She started acting less like my cousin and more like an authority figure. She still viewed me as a little girl, but it was time she realized that I was a woman and could make my own decisions. All of the little hiccups she and I had made me avoid her even more. I didn't feel wanted.

Megan and I had been talking casually one day, and I told her that I was thinking about becoming full time at Comcast and quitting Walmart which upset her because she was the one who helped me get the job.

"Did you text Evan and tell him that you are quitting? You should text him and let him know that you are leaving, at least give him a heads up... You only got that job because of me", she reminded me.

So much for support. How did me saying I'm thinking about quitting turn into this?

A few days later, I was at work and Evan came up to me.

"I heard that you are quitting. When are you putting in your two weeks? Your cousin texted me saying that you'd be quitting.

She thanked me for giving you the opportunity and told me that working two jobs was too much for you. I know you did it for me and I just wanted to say thank you".

Furious couldn't even describe my feelings at that moment. How could she cross the line like that? I hadn't even made up my mind yet.

I apologized to Evan who ironically, was planning to leave the job soon himself, and explained the situation to him. He was understanding, but that was the last straw for me. It was time for me to go back home. I was going to pack up my things without saying anything and get on with my life.

My first phone call was to Lish. I updated her on everything that was going on and informed her that I was moving back home. She kindly offered to book a flight in order to help me drive back home and she also offered me a place to stay once we reached Philadelphia so that I didn't have to move back in with my parents. After I established my concrete plans for the coming weeks and my move, I felt at ease. Everything was falling into place.

Calling Liam was the next thing on my list. Per our conversation, he seemed really happy that I was moving back, especially because he knew about all the drama that had transpired between me and Megan.

The next day while I was at work, Lish texted me, asking if I had talked to Liam, which I hadn't. When I asked her why, she was hesitant to tell me because I was working, but she finally caved.

"Why did Liam's baby mom call my phone earlier, and we were going back and forth and I'm mad at myself for even going there with her because she is not worth it... You know me and Liam text here and there, checking on one another, and I had texted him asking how he was feeling because he told me he felt sick... Sam why I get a phone call! I'm like hello, and all she said was, "is this Sam?".

As always, I was beside myself.

Lish continued with her recount. "So, then she said, "Why are you texting Liam? How do you know him? He has a girlfriend. Stop calling and texting his phone! I will beat you up if you keep texting him!"", and my response was "You're not going to beat nobody up. You don't want to fight me. I will hurt you. You don't even know who you are talking too!"

I couldn't apologize to Lish enough, and the fact that Liam didn't contact me to inform me of what happened upset me even more. Lish told me that he'd sent her a message apologizing, stating that he didn't know what to say to me.

"Lish, let's see if he texts me. He hasn't yet… But thank you for telling me". I thanked her again for being such a good friend to me, and then I hung up because I had to get back to work.

Working and waiting, I was curious to see how long it would take for Liam to text me, but the text never came. As always, I took the initiative and reached out to him first.

"Is there something you want to tell me?"

"You talked to Lish?"

"That wasn't my question".

"Yes, I have to tell you something… Ka'maya went through my phone, saw me texting Lish, and decided to call her and start some mess for no reasons at all. I texted Lish telling her that I was sorry and that won't ever happen again".

That's all he said. No details whatsoever. I wanted to know more about why this happened, how this happened, and why he didn't tell me before Lish did.

"Liam, this is not cool at all. The fact that your baby mom has access to your phone and calling my best friend coming at her… Lish has nothing to do with this. If your phone is locked, why does she know the code? Not only that, but she's been playing on my phone too".

There was a brief pause

"She said you had a girlfriend. Just be upfront with me Liam, are you two back together? I don't need this extra drama. You have been distant lately. I have been playing it cool until now"

"Samantha, there is nothing going on between me and Ka'maya. We are not together. I am with you. She is mad because I told her that me and you are together so now she is playing on your phone and calling Lish and the only reason why she said something with Lish because she probably doesn't know if the number she is calling is yours or not", was his response.

I knew he was lying, but I was beginning to think that maybe he didn't know the difference between the truth and a lie.

"Samantha I gotta go. I can't really talk right now... I am going to call you back later".

When I got off of work, I called him, and of course he didn't answer. I called once more, but it went to voicemail. I wasn't even going to bother texting him. I was over it.

I didn't hear from him for the rest of the night, and I was mad but this time, I wasn't going to let it get to me. I was already stressed with everything else going on in my life, and the last thing I needed to be doing was worrying about Liam.

He Facetimed me the next day. I shared with him how I was feeling about the relationship being too hard and that I was tired of dealing with the drama.

"I understand. Last night, I didn't answer your call because me and Ka'maya got into it. I told her that she could keep the place and I left... She wants to act like she is my girlfriend but we're not together, and she wants to question me, so I packed my stuff up and I left. I am back at my mom's house".

Is he telling the truth?

"Sam, I know I lied to you in the past, but I am not lying to you now. I am glad that I moved out, because now that you're coming back, we can actually be together. I am going to have my own place and you will be over every day. I swear on my daughter I am not still dealing with my baby mom. I am with you. I love you Samantha and I am not going to lose you"

Would he swear on his daughter if he was lying? I wasn't sure what to think about him, us or anything anymore.

Our conversation drifted away from the issue at hand and he asked if I was excited to come home… The answer was no, but I had to do what I had to do. The thought of leaving Atlanta was bittersweet, but life happens, and Megan and I could not live under the same roof any longer. I did have two coworkers who offered to let me live with them until I figured everything out, but I decided it was best to chalk my experience up to being a "lesson learned", and to return home.

My plan was to interview for my old position at SPIN as soon as I got back so that I could save money for my own apartment, but my more immediate plans were still up in the air. I wasn't sure if I was going to tell Megan that I was leaving or not, but ultimately made the decision not to. I only had few more days until I was back in Philadelphia and I wanted my last few days to be peaceful, fun, and drama free.

Not long before my departure, Megan came down into the basement and noticed that all of my stuff was packed up.

"Sam are you moving?", she asked.

"Yes, I am going back home".

"And you weren't going to tell me? When did you decide this?"

The look on her face changed suddenly, and I knew she was bothered by the fact that I hadn't mentioned it. In an effort to avoid further contention, I changed the subject. She was now on a need to know basis and I didn't feel that she needed to know anything beyond the fact that I was leaving.

Lish's flight landed at the perfect time, giving me an excuse to leave and evade an even more awkward situation with Megan. During our ride, I filled her in on everything that had transpired between us and she was just as surprised as I was.

We got back to the house and it seemed that Megan was waiting for us.

Not knowing what to say, I asked if she'd remembered Lish.

"Yes of course I remember her! Hey Lish! Give me a hug! How are you?", she asked.

"I'm good, how are you?", Lish responded, matching her energy.

"You came down to visit Samantha before she heads back home? You know she is moving back right?" She responded.

Lish just played it off, "Yeah! Had to come visit Atlanta before she left for Philly".

In my head, all I could think about was how Megan constantly ran her mouth... What if I didn't want Lish to know that I was moving?

That night, Lish and I ended up going out to Lips Drag Queen Show Palace where we had a blast, and the night after, it was time for me to go. Lish helped me pack my things in the car as we got set to leave.

"Wait, Sam, you're not going to say anything to Megan at all about you leaving tonight?", she asked.

"No, I am not going to say anything to her. I am leaving her a note. I am over her and the fact we were crashing Lish, I am hurt! I am hurt that it even came to this. She was my favorite cousin... I looked up to her, but now I see her for who she really is. This whole 360 hurt me...I was happy to be living with her. She was like my big sister, and now I don't know. I am shocked".

"Sam, I know you are hurt, but don't be petty. She was nice enough to let you stay with her. Don't leave without saying bye. The fact is, she knows that you're leaving, but don't know that you're leaving tonight. Just say bye"

Because I'm stubborn, I wasn't going to budge. I'd intended to leave a note, but God has a funny way of working. I realized not long after we pulled off that I had left my house keys behind. Not only did I have no choice but to turn back around, but I also needed her to let me in the house since all of my keys were on the same ring.

"Megan, I am sorry that I didn't tell you I was leaving tonight and that I didn't tell you that I was leaving all together. Thank you for opening up your home to me, letting me stay with you, and giving me the opportunity to even live in Atlanta. I love you. Thank you for all that you've done for me, and again sorry for not staying goodbye the right way".

"I love you too baby girl. Have a safe trip back home and text me so that I know that you and Lish made it home safe"

I gave both Megan and Jamir a hug, said goodbye, and then we left.

My SPIN interview was the next day and thankfully, I got the job. During my first day of training, Liam sent me a text from an unknown number... Apparently, he'd broken his phone a few weeks prior when he was in North Carolina.

Why was he in North Carolina and didn't mention it?

And then suddenly, I remembered that that's where Ka'maya was originally from.

That night, he invited me to dinner for a face to face conversation at Las Margaritas, and he broke up with me.

"Sam, I love you. I am in love with you... I swear on my daughter that I love you, but I am not the man for you, and it wouldn't be fair to put you through all of this. I am in love with you and I want to be with you, you make me beyond happy. The way you make me feel, I've never felt this way about anyone before. You treat me like a man", was how the conversation began.

"Okay, if you feel this way why are you ending things? That doesn't make sense to me". I was beyond the point of confusion.

His explanation was long-winded and not believable in the least, but it ended by him telling me that he loved me, but he was going to be with Ka'maya as he wanted to give their daughter a two-parent household she deserved.

I started to cry. "Why can't you be happy with me? Why can't you choose me? Why can't you choose happiness! You are just making yourself unhappy in the long run. You'd rather choose to be in a relationship that makes you miserable than being with someone who makes you happy?"

"...Can we still be friends?", he asked.

"No, we can't! I don't want to be your friend… Lose my number! Goodbye Liam".

I wanted to throw my drink in his face. I couldn't believe what was happening… All I could do is cry. I was only back home for two weeks and he broke up with me after telling me how excited he was to have me back home. I opened up my heart to him once again, and he did the same thing. My brother was right. If Liam taught me anything, it was that love is a gamble. He'd been with his baby mom the whole time, and the fact I was back home messed up everything for him so he had no choice but to leave me.

Coinciding scriptures

CREATE IN ME a pure heart, God and make my spirit right again. Do not send me away from you or take your Holy Spirit away from me. Give me back the joy of your salvation. Keep me strong by giving me a willing spirit. (Psalms 51:10-12 NCV)

THE WISE WOMAN builds her house, but with her own hands foolish one tears her hers down. Whoever fears the Lord walks uprightly, but those who despise him are devious in their ways. (Proverbs 14:1-2 NIV)

GUIDE ME IN your truth and teach me, for you are God my savior, and my hope is in you all day long. (Psalms 25:5 NIV)

CHAPTER 11

Same Old Drama...
Time to Let Go of The Past

GOD IS MY person "My person" …the person you go to for every-thing, the person you can't live without, the person you stay mad at, and the person that supports you in everything that you do. Being someone's "person" is a commitment!!

COINED FROM MY favorite show, 'Grey's Anatomy'

"MY PERSON"

Beyoncé's Lemonade album was my theme song for a while. I could not stop listening to it when it first came out, especially because it felt so relevant. My favorite three songs were "Hold Up", "Sorry", and "Pray You Catch Me", Tamar Braxton was on repeat too "Pieces", "Never", "Circles", and "Broken Record". I felt like a woman scorned; filled with anger, hurt, pain, envy, jealousy, and betrayal. How could I be so stupid and open myself up to Liam again? I knew he was a liar the whole time, but I still stayed with him. As much as I tried to convince myself that he'd changed, he hadn't.

The ordeal with Liam filled me with so much misery that I purposely kept myself busy with work to keep my mind off of him and the situation. And whenever I wasn't able to so easily take my mind off of him, all I could think about was getting revenge.

Don't sin by letting anger control you. Think about it overnight and remain silent ~Psalm 4:4 NLT.

Slowly but surely, I got myself together. I wasn't going to allow my rage to consume me. Afterall, it was his loss, not mine. I deserved much better… It had been about 3 weeks since the breakup and Liam started texting me again. However, this time I was ignoring him. I stuck to my guns and was adamant about my stance until he sent me a picture of his car with the windows broken out. *Did he think I did it?* I had to call him to clear the air.

"I know you didn't do it. I just wanted to show you what my car looks like. Ka'maya did this to my car", he said.

"Wow. She did that? For what?" I asked him.

"Because she was looking for you, she came over here like a mad woman running all through the house talking about "where is Sam? I know she is here'".

What would make her think that I was there? Him and I didn't even speak anymore. And what did he want me to do? He did choose to be with her so why should I feel bad for him. Did he think by telling me that she was jealous of me would make me happy? I could care less! What part of "I don't want to be friends" did he not understand?

He tried to lure me back in with messages about how much he missed me and that he wished he would have chosen me and I know he sent me the photo to make me feel bad for him just like he'd done when he told me about his mom's heart attack.

"Can we start over?", he asked.

"No, we can't. I'm sorry, but you hurt me, and I won't allow you to hurt me again. You not going to do anything but lie to me again. I told you I don't want to be a part of the toxic love triangle that is for you and Ka'maya to have. You want me now that you don't have me, but once you and your baby mom make up, I am back on the block list. So, no. Not this time around. I don't choose you this time, I choose me."

"Sam I am not lying I am telling you the truth."

From then on, me and Liam started texting each other again, but only as friends. No matter what he did to me, I couldn't shake him off. I knew that I wasn't going to get back with him though, but even after all he'd done, I wasn't ready for him to leave my life completely.

One day after we made plans to hang out, we went to Liam's house to hang out and I made it a point not to stay long because I didn't want to give him the wrong impression… From that night on, he and I only texted sporadically, and it was only when he texted me first. With no explanation, he blocked my number again, so I ended up telling him to leave me alone and to delete my number. That was pretty much the end of our relationship as I'd known it.

It didn't take long for him to attempt to come back in my life again though. One Sunday, he'd popped up at my parents' house saying how much he missed me and really wished that we could be friends.

Here we go again.

The conversation didn't last long, and he left with his head hung low. This time, I was not budging.

A few weeks before my birthday, I got a call from Ka'maya. She found my number in his call-log and was calling around to ask who was calling her boyfriend. When I told her who I was, she asked if we could talk woman to woman.

"That depends. Are we actually going to talk, women to women? Because if not, then no we cannot talk", I responded curtly.

"Yes, we are actually going to talk because I am confused about how you and Liam are in contact and I know if I ask him he is going to lie because he is a liar, and now that you are on the phone I can get some answers… I'm confused though because he has your number in his phone under Samuel".

If my name was under Samuel then why is she on the phone with me now?

Then began the interrogation. I answered what felt like a million questions about myself, about Liam, and about the true nature of our relationship.

After the questioning ceased, she began to reveal some truths about Liam that I had been ignorant to. She revealed that they'd never broken up, that his family loved her, that he'd gotten us the same exact Christmas gifts, and that he only came to see me in Atlanta because she had had sex with someone else in their bed... He'd also told Ka'maya that I was ugly and called me his side-chick... She knew where I lived currently and that I'd recently moved back from Atlanta, that I'd given him money, everything. And what made it worse was that the money I had given him to help him get out the hole he was in, he had giving it to her to go shopping.

I was pissed. After all that I'd been through and shared with him, he was never really there for me. Ever!

And then she got into the story about why she busted his car windows. Turns out, his brother had told Ka'maya that I was there at the house and she knew that I bought their daughter tickets to see Disney on Ice even though he tried to pass it off like he had been the one to buy them.

After all of that, she had the nerve to say to me that I could have him, but Liam was the furthest thing from my mind. I was more than happy to be out of their games and out this toxic love triangle.

"The funny thing is I thought that he'd changed and he was going to do right this time around. We even started to go to church together. If it wasn't for me, he would not have the job he has. My dad got him that job he is at now", she said.

Why was she telling me all of this? I just wanted to finally hear the truth.

"Matter of fact, I am going to call him on 3-way... You don't mind, do you? That way we can put all this to an end".

Before I got a chance to answer, she'd clicked over and called Liam.

"Liam I am confused, are you messing with Sam?", she said without hesitation.

" No, Ka'maya I am not messing with her. Why do you keep asking me about Sam? I do not know her?" he responded.

"Oh so now you don't know me?", I cut in.

"No, I don't. Who are you?" He really tried to keep the charade going. Even after I mentioned him having my number, coming to see me the week prior, etc., he still tried to play it off.

"Don't try and play me! You a whole nut and I don't know what I ever saw in you, you are not a man you are a boy. A grown boy and I wished I never met you and if you were on fire, I wouldn't even spit on you to save you. You don't exist to me", and I hung up the phone.

Fuming, I got in the shower after the call, in order to calm myself down. When I got out, I'd had so many missed calls... 5 from Liam and 3 from Ka'maya.

I ignored Liam's called Ka'maya back.

" Liam wants to talk to you", she said.

"For what? I have nothing to say". But before I knew it, Liam was on the phone.

"Bitch! Who the fuck you think you are calling my girl, coming at her?"

Silence.

"You could never replace my girl. She looks better than you. You are ugly and dirty. I used you for everything. I used you for the money, Disney On Ice tickets, XBox, sex, everything. You are good for nothing, your sex is corny, the only thing that you are good for is laying on your back. Who could ever want to be with you? Nobody. Even niggas call your phone just to have sex with you and they know your sex is whack".

At that moment, I knew it was him and Ka'maya playing on my phone a while back. One of them was pretending to be someone else named Brandon, saying that they'd met me at the Chinese store. I knew I didn't recognize the name and I didn't even frequent the store I'd apparently met him at. I let it go at the time, but I should've put two and two together. The foolery. They'd been playing me for months and I didn't even know.

Liam continued, "They know your pussy stink too. You could never look better than my girl, you don't dress better than her, you can't dress, your breath stink, you broke, fuck you, and you're an ugly ass bitch!

I hung up in tears.

Did he just say that to me? How did I stay on the phone and listen to him say all of that to me?

I was feeling the lowest I'd felt in a long while. Someone that I loved said all of this to me so effortlessly all because he got caught? And the fact that Ka'maya could just sit on the phone and listen to him bothered me just as much

I had to call Lish and tell her what had happened. I was still shocked and to make matters worse, I had to get ready for work.

Lish was surprised once she heard all that Liam said to me and told me that him and I needed to be done and for good this time. She threatened to end our friendship if I ever talked to him again, so I knew she was serious.

As iron sharpens iron, so a friend sharpens a friend ~Proverbs 27:17.

"Honestly Sam. I believe that this was God's way of getting you out of that! You were hindering your worth by being with him. You were treating him the way you wanted to be treated. You had blinders on. God was giving you sign after sign, but because you had blinders on you couldn't see it". The devil has many faces and he was the enemy in disguise!

I prayed, and I prayed I found the truth beneath his lies. I prayed to the Lord that he revealed what his truth was, and God did just that, but I ignored every sign, every step of the way.

The saying, "sticks and stones may break my bones, but words will never hurt me", did not ring true in this case. Liam's words hurt and they cut me deep.

How could someone I cared so much for say these things to me? I did not nothing but stay in his corner and try to help him better himself. How could he come at me and my character like that?

Thinking back on it, it wasn't just that Liam blatantly disrespected me, belittled me, made me feel like I was nothing, it was the fact that I told him that most of my exes had also played me and disrespected me and he promised that he wouldn't do that to me and he did. Liam was the devil in disguise. He was the same as all my other exes, just with a different identity.

I channeled my energy into different, more important things, and though it took a while, it eventually started working. I had finally found an apartment, I just needed to save up some more money to get everything in order. My move in date was for October 15th. Everything was coming together beautifully and I remained focused on moving on with my life and strengthening my relationship with God.

During my healing process, I was looking for something. Something greater to fill my void, my open wounds, my feeling of lack, my thoughts of not being good enough, but what needed was spiritual healing and the only person who completely satisfied my soul was God. He healed me from the bondage and pain and still healing parts of me. He gave me peace that surpasses all understanding that I still do not understand. He showed himself to be my healer, my deliverer, my redeemer, my restorer, my way maker, my breakthrough, my way out, and if God wasn't "my person" during my healing journey, I wouldn't be able to say, "I am whole, I am enough, I am loved."
~Samantha Williams

Lessons

*H*OLD STRONG IN *the Lord, no matter what you are going through. No matter what the world throws at you, God will give you His strength to endure.* ~*Samantha Williams*

*W*HEN THE ENEMY *TRIES to attack, it's because he's trying to block a blessing God has for you. Keep pushing through.* ~*Alisha Curry*

~*A* GOOD PERSON *produces good things from the treasury of a good heart, and an evil person produces evil things from the treasury of an evil heart. What you say flows from what is in your heart* –*Luke 6:45 NLT*~

CHAPTER 12

Let Go and Let God!

THE MOMENT YOU become obedient to the calling over your life is when God will cause opportunities to line up that will change your life ~Alisha Curry.

After what felt like forever, I finally moved into my new apartment, and not only did I move successfully, I had also rededicated my life back to Christ. I needed a change and I wanted to break free from the chains that were holding me down.

I started reading the bible and going back to church every Saturday. And Lish helped me a lot as well, sending me a few books like, "The Submissive Wife", "Sex, Lies, & Soul Ties", "SNARE", "Wise Her Still", "Wisdom for the Wait", and "Basic Elements of the Christian Life".

The more I read, the heavier my prayers got… The prayer that stuck out to me the most, the one I can recall so vividly reads as follows:

> *"Father God, I am calling on you. I am crying out to you. Please Father hear my cry. I ask you Father God, to fill the void that I am feeling and release me from my soul ties. I need you in my life. I do not want to go on my own, but instead do things your way. I am lost out here and I need you to guide me. I need your love and only your love so that I may know what love is. Father God,*

teach me my worth, give me strength, courage, under-standing, love, hope, and peace. Protect me under your wings, I beg you Father, please take this pain that I have and endure me with your Holy Spirit… Teach me to show people my heart and have them love me for my heart and my internal beauty and not just my body. If anyone comes my way that was not sent by you, please rebuke it. Somewhere along the way I told myself that I wasn't enough. I don't know if it was the relationship I was in, the disappointments I'd had in others and myself, being told that I was not smart enough, pretty enough, good enough, etc. I really started to believe that I wasn't enough over the years. I lacked confidence, self-worth, and I continue to do things to please everyone around me. I felt like a failure. Help me Father. In the name of Jesus, Amen".

Not long after, I got a text from Lish and that read, "You are enough! God made you unique for a reason. You have something to contribute to this world and that's enough in itself. You're not your past, you're not a failure, you're not the person who was tore you down. You are you, the person who's enough in God's eyes–That's how you should view yourself… having and being Enough. Be intentional in Prayer time, asking God to help you through. Beat depression and the anxiety you got from feeling like you're not enough because you are! Use Prayer, Meditation and Godfirmations…they really do work"

When I read that message, my eyes welled with tears… Lish had no idea that I had just prayed, asking God for the validation that she's just given me. I knew that that was God speaking directly to me through Lish. All I could say was, "thank you Lord".

The Lord says, I will guide you along the best pathways for your life. I will advise you and watch over you. ~Psalms 32:8 NLT

Lish and her cousin Tiana became my accountability sisters during my journey to Christ. We meet up to read the word, to pray and to hold each other accountable for the things that were going on around us and give each other advice.

Since I'd rededicated my life back to Christ, everything has fallen into place. Between moving, getting all of my furniture, and getting a second job, I finally felt like my life was making some progress and that I was on the right track. I am so thankful for the people that God placed in my life and for the ones that he removed as well. I changed my lifestyle for the better and let him do his work.

I've learned that whenever you start to overcome your struggles, it seems that the devil will try to knock you off your mark. The day of my housewarming, I got an Instagram message from Ka'maya, wondering if Liam and I were talking again.

I showed the message to Lish in disbelief.

"Are you kidding me? The fact that she has to even message you to ask you that is embarrassing. If you have to check up on your man like that then why be with him? That is too much... That means that he is not her man. She's playing herself.... Are you going to reply?"

"Yea, I am writing to her now".

"Honestly, I have not talked to him since we were all on the phone and I don't have any intention of speaking to him. Respectfully, I would appreciate it if you leave me out of the drama and leave me alone", I wrote to her.

She apologized and promised not to message me again. I was proud of how much I'd grown. I really had no intention in talking to him and I was ready to move on. That situation is in God's hands... I've learned that you reap what you sow. God was going to handle them in his own time and in his own way.

I was happy on the inside out–Your beauty shouldn't come from outward adornment. It should be your inner self, the unfading beauty of a gentle spirit.

A month later, Liam tried to reach out again. He apologized to me, stating that he missed me and was still in love with me… I screenshot that email, sent it to Lish, and then I deleted it. Was this a joke? I couldn't do anything but laugh.

Jesus give me the strength to survive.

It was New Year's Day, 2017, and Liam emailed me again saying "Happy New Year", that he missed me, and asking me if we could talk.

"Liam. Please leave me alone. I have nothing else to say to you. You did what you did… You made your bed, now lie in it. Don't email me anymore and stop saying you love me because you don't. If you did you would have NEVER disrespected me like that. I saw a side to you that I didn't like, but that was your true self. You meant every word that you said… I felt it! Just like a drunk person speaks a sober mind, so does a mad person. That is why they say be careful of what you say when you are mad because there are some things you cannot take back and in some way that is exactly how you really felt. The tongue is a dangerous weapon. I forgive you for what you did, what you said, but me and you could never be friends again. Goodbye Liam",

A couple of weeks later, he emailed me again asking If I could call him because he knew that I changed my number. Because he had no way to contact me via phone, he ended up sending me a plethora of emails instead. I couldn't understand why he was sending me emails after he disrespected me the way he had.

One night during an overnight shift, I ended up calling him to hear what he had to say, however I blocked my number so that he couldn't get my new number.

"Hello Liam, what do you want? Why do you keep emailing me?"

"Do you know how good it feels to hear your voice right now Samantha? I miss you so much. How are you?"

I couldn't believe he had the audacity to act like nothing had happened.

"Don't ask me how I am doing".

"Samantha I am sorry. To think about how I hurt you over and over again, it hurts me to know that I hurt you. You were my everything and I am thinking how could I allow myself to get this mad and hurt the woman that I love so badly. What I said to you was not me. I thought that you and Ka'maya were teaming up on me… I was caught, and the only way out was to hurt you and that killed me on the inside to say that to you. It is still killing me… I want to apologize to your mom and dad. They were nothing but nice to me and I disrespected their daughter. They didn't deserve that".

Conversation ensued and I decided that it was best that I forgive the situation because that's what Jesus would do. I was over myself, especially because after that night, Liam and I started talking again, but I didn't tell anyone except Kylie. I knew I couldn't tell Lish. I was upset at myself because how could I let him back into my life? After everything that happened, why would I let him back? I move on with God and here I am going backwards. God removed Liam from my life and here I am listening to the enemy by opening the door again… It seemed like the moment I let Liam back in, everything started falling out of place, both in my personal and my professional life. I stopped getting as much overtime at work, which meant that my bills also started piling up, and I wasn't sure if I'd be able to renew my lease due to rent prices. Everything was going so well before Liam came back in my life, but living a life of dishonesty proved to be my downfall.

He and I decided that it was best that we hash everything out face to face, so we set up a time for him to come over to my house to do just that. He explained his side of the story stating that "things aren't always what they seem", but I could feel in my gut that he was lying.

One day, not long after that conversation, Liam and I went to the beach for the day and when I dropped him off at his house, he noticed that Ka'maya was there with their daughter, just waiting for him to come home. When he noticed her, he started to drive off and she followed us.

"What are you doing?" I asked him

" Getting away from Ka'maya", he responded. " I am not putting you in anymore drama with her and I am not letting you fight her"

Liam was speeding to get away from her. It was almost like we were on a highway speed chase. He was even more pissed that she was doing this while their daughter was in the back seat of the car.

In that moment I thought to myself, "why am I doing this? I am going through this all over again, and it's not even worth it. I need to let Liam go. Here I am, in a speed chase with his baby mom".

When Liam finally lost her, he got out of the car to walk home and told me to go home myself. Later that day, he called me to apologize. I was such a fool for falling for this again.. I had just found God and learned my self-worth. Why would I go backwards for a man that's not worth it and was not willing to put me first? I moved on from him, and I need to continue to move on from him... This will only hurt me in the end.

The same day I received countless messages on Instagram from Ka'maya, but I blocked her. And once she realized that I blocked her, she contacted me through her friends account. I blocked that one too.

I had no intention of fighting over a guy. Never have. Never will.

One day I was in the store and my phone rang. I thought it was Liam calling me, but it was Ka'maya saying that Liam had a girlfriend and stop to stop calling his phone.

Here we go again.

All of the drama was too much and I started to fall back off of Liam. I couldn't take it anymore… The lies, the deceit, and the run arounds were all too much for me to handle.

Liam told me that he was going to Jamaica for 3 weeks with his family. He asked me to go with him, but I did not want to go. The day after he left for Jamaica, Ka'maya called me. I don't know how she did it, but she managed to get my phone number.

"Umm Samantha, I am trying to figure out how and why you are talking to Liam after all that happened? I am not going anywhere and if you are going to be with him I am going to make your life a living hell. You are going to have to deal with me because I am not going anywhere".

"That is fine. I am over you two. Lose my number because I am walking away", I said.

"Good, because I don't want to have to fight you... I don't want to have to call you again Samantha".

"Bye Ka'maya. You can have the petty drama", and that was it.

A few weeks later, Lish, my mom, and I went to DC with the church to visit the African American Museum. That night when we returned home, me and Lish were in the car and I was telling her about Liam and the phone conversation with Ka'maya.

"I am not going to lie, I had the feeling you were going to start talking to him again. Ka'maya basically told you that she was not going anywhere... And I am not letting you fight over a guy. He is not worth it, none of them are worth it. Let her have him and she can deal with the drama, toxic, and the lies. That is not a relationship worth fighting for or a relationship that you should or would want. They can have each other... You deserve so much more. Your King is coming. God is just getting him out of a situation that he needs to get out of and getting y'all ready for each other", Lish affirmed me.

The next morning when I left out for work, I found my car keyed and my tires slashed... At that moment, I knew it was Ka'maya who did this to my car. All I could see was red. I was so heated and filled with rage. I wanted to go to his house and bust the windows out of his car just to get to Ka'maya. I wanted to fight her. I wanted to get all the information I could about her so that I could beat the daylights out of her. Thankfully Lish and Tiana was able to calm me down, but Lish, also had to calm herself down too. I was pissed, but I called my dad who called AAA, and we got my car towed to a car shop to get new tires and also made a police report. That was it. The last straw,

Once again, this was God's way of opening my eyes and allowing me to see that I needed to leave Liam alone for good. When you don't listen, he will take drastic measures to ensure that you do.

GOD HAS PUT you in this difficult situation so that you can grow. Trust this process and stay prayed up. Rejoice in our confident hope. Be patient in trouble and keep on praying -Romans 12:12 NLT

"Sam, I swear on everything after this you better be done! You should have been done before, but after this situation you better be done! This has gone too far now, and I don't want to see you hurt this girl yet alone me hurt this little girl she had some serious growing up to do. I will slap the crap out of you if you start talking to him again, I promise you, you will lose me as a friend because I can't sit here and watch you go through this. You deserve so much more! So much better! You want a God-fearing man, someone who will love you, be there for you, support you, hold you up, uplift you, and so much more", Lish told me.

Once again, I knew she meant it.

When Liam came home from Jamaica, I didn't hear from him at all. NOTHING! Not even to say that he heard what happened while he was away.

I cried out to God again, asking him for strength where I was weak, for guidance and understanding, and for my spirit to take over and not my emotions.

"Help me Father, help me to stay true to myself and to say true to you. To let you lead and I follow. You are my shepherd. I shall not want. Help me to resist the devil so that he may flee from me".

My birthday had rolled around again, and my cousin was taking me out for dinner later that night. When I opened the door, there was a card and flowers there waiting for me.

"Sam, I am sorry that you didn't hear from me after I got back home. I miss you so much. Being with you makes me happy and I do not want to lose you. I want to be your future husband, and to start a family with you. I want you to be my misses. I know that I keep making mistake after mistake and it makes you question me. Please give me another chance", the card read.

I threw everything in the trash. Liam was now in God's hands.

I left Liam and Ka'maya in my past and I moved on. It was time that I started putting God and myself first.

Time has gone by and I am no longer allowing my past to dictate my future. Where God wants me to go and where God wants me to be is where I want to go as well. I am still on my walk and letting him lead the way as I continue to walk by faith and not by sight.

Liam still emails me, messaged me and calls me from time to time, but I finally blocked him from everything so now there is no way that he can get in touch with me… I guess it's true what they say, you never know what you have until it's gone. I have grown and learned from every situation that I've been in and I will continue to hold my head up high as God shines his light on me. I pray it shines so bright that when people see me, they see God through me.

DON'T BE AFRAID, for I am with you. Don't be discouraged for I am your God. I will strengthen you and help you. I will hold you up with my victorious right hand. (Isaiah 41:10 NLT)

I prayed and asked God to send me a God-Fearing Man that I can grow with, build with, learn from, pray with, worship with, and God did just that. I kept on asking, praying, and seeking, and God brought him to me. A man, my husband, my soulmate… Funny thing is, I've known him all along. His name is Thibaut Azondekon.

KEEP ON ASKING, and you will receive what you ask for. Keep on seeking, and you will find. Keep on knocking, and the door will be opened to you. For everyone who asks, receives. Everyone who seeks, finds. And to everyone who knocks the door will be opened (Matthew 7:8 NLT)

To be continued... **Life After the Storm**

GOD WILL ALLOW you to go through the same things over and over again until you learn the lesson behind it – Alisha Curry

CHAPTER 13

Godfirmation

I WILL NEVER let anyone shame me of my past. When you are in a new space in life, the first thing people try to do is shame you with who you were in the past or what you've done in the past. But you are more than the choices that you've made. God has forgiven your past, so it's not a part of God's plan for you to stay living there.
~Samantha Williams

Behind every successful woman there's a gang of onlookers who swear they can tell her story better than her. Truth is no one can tell her story better than her! She's the only one that has lived it… They call it success; she calls it BLESSING! They believe materials are signs of being successful. She believes spiritual growth is true success!

These 4 rules are what helped me live a life of total freedom.

1. Change your lifestyle. (Renew your mindset) Romans 12:2
2. Surrender it all to God. (Allow God to fill your voids) Colossians 2:10
3. Release your past. (Forgive yourself & others as God forgive) Colossians 3:13
4. Freely choose joy & happiness (Enjoy God's peace that surpasses all understanding) Philippians 4:7

5. Meditate on the scriptures provided that you need healing in. (Remember that this is a journey so your healing process will take some time. Every day that you work towards it with God's help will make it one day closer to your freedom) ~Alisha Curry

"GOD GLOW" WHEN you are all about God, depend on God, and always reaching for God. You exude a Glow from God. – Alisha Curry

"FOR I KNOW the plans I have for you," says the Lord. "They are plans for good and not disaster, to give you a future and hope. ~Jeremiah 29:11